YES YES LIVING IN A NO NO WORLD

YES YES LIVING IN A NO NO WORLD

by
Neil Eskelin

Logos International
Plainfield, New Jersey

YES YES LIVING IN A NO NO WORLD
Copyright © 1980 by Logos International
All rights reserved
Printed in the United States of America
Library of Congress Catalog Card Number: 80-80914
International Standard Book Number: 0-88270-417-6
Logos International, Plainfield, New Jersey 07060

To my son, Ian

Introduction

Some time ago I took a sheet of paper and divided it into two columns: "*Yes* People," and "*No* People." Then I thought about people I knew and wrote their names in the appropriate column. And what a shock it was to see the length of the "No" list.

These were people who heard someone say, "You can't do that!" and they believed it. Now they were saying, "It can't be done!" and were affecting the lives of others.

If your friends made such a list right now, under which heading would they write your name? What do they say about you?

This book was written with the firm belief that you can say goodbye to the No No world forever. Yes, in *every* situation, you can respond with *hope* instead of fear, with *encouragement*, instead of criticism, with *belief* instead of despair.

We're going to talk about your actions, your attitudes,

your words, and your objectives. And I believe that you can begin right now to live a brand new life!

My parents gave me a great example of Yes Yes living. *I tried it and it works!* And now I want to share it with you.

I wish that every young person could be guided by the principles you're about to read. What a world this would be! If you know someone who needs what this book is all about, please give him a copy.

Now, let's begin. *Your "stop lights" are about to change from red to green.*

Contents

YES YES
LIVING
IN A
NO NO
WORLD

The Miracle of
Yes Yes Living!

You are about to experience a new level of living. It is a life known to only a fraction of our world. But those who have discovered it have found a never-ending source of personal energy, expectancy, motivation and love.

Somewhere in the pages of this book it will suddenly happen to you! "Yes Yes living" will become more than a phrase. More than thinking. More than speaking. More than acting. It will become a permanent part of your very life. Yes, a part of your heart, your soul, your spirit.

Just think for a moment of the people you know and you'll realize that the overwhelming majority of humanity live in a "No No" world. They "can't." They "won't." They "don't." And their life is a cycle of criticism and complaint.

But we weren't born that way. As children we rode on magic carpets and built castles made of sand.

At one time we were all like the children in the second-grade class who were asked to write about their parents. Here's how little Danny saw his dad: "He can climb the highest mountain or swim the biggest ocean. He can fly the fastest plane and fight the strongest tiger. My father can do anything. But most of the time he just carries out the garbage."

What a commentary on life! "He just carries out the garbage." Danny described the daily routine of millions. Just dealing with today's trash.

It's time for some fresh air. Yes, you really *can* climb lofty mountains and fight life's tigers. *You really can!*

YES, IT'S A MIRACLE

I always enjoy telling people about the positive thinker who fell out of the window on the seventeenth floor of the World Trade Center in New York. Every time he passed a floor people recalled hearing him saying, "So far, so good."

Obviously, he needed more than good thoughts.

You may ask, "What is the difference between positive thinking and Yes Yes living? Aren't they really the same?"

There *is* a difference that can best be described as the difference between *thinking* and *living*. I am a great believer in positive thinking and put it into practice every day. But Yes Yes living expands the boundaries. It deals with action, with feeling, with being, with speaking, with living. Yes, with *living*.

You Can Change the Atmosphere

The miracle of Yes Yes living is that it affects *every-*

thing you do. In fact, it even changes the *atmosphere*. That's right! You can walk into a room and people will instantly know there is something special about you.

When I am driving to speaking engagements and it's time to eat, I usually look for the restaurant with the biggest crowd. Something must be attracting them. Recently, in Birmingham, I saw a packed parking lot and pulled in. The building wasn't attractive, the menu was average and the food was nothing to put in a cookbook. But the atmosphere inside was electric. Everybody seemed to be having a super time. Complete strangers were talking to each other. It was loud, but it certainly was fun. In fact, my waitress walked up and said, "Hi, I'm Jodi! What's *your* name?" Well, it was quite a restaurant.

Paying my check, I complimented the manager on the good service and the friendly waitresses. And I'll never forget his reply.

"Mister," he said in his slow Southern drawl, "I just have one rule around here. I only hire gals who like people. If they can't laugh and joke with the customers, I fire 'em."

It worked miracles for his business. And the secret was so simple.

The building didn't do it.

The location didn't do it.

The menu didn't do it.

People did it. People who really liked people. That made the difference.

But think for a moment of a time when there were no people. The world was pitch black. It was empty. And

God said, "Let there be light." Then the miracles multiplied and man was created. Yes, a living, breathing, loving creature. It was *very* good. And suddenly there was Yes Yes living in a No No world.

And the miracle is still happening. Darkness is still turning to light. Despair is still turning to hope. Defeat is still turning to victory.

It Starts Right Where You Are

Unfortunately, millions of people think they've got to be "Number One" before they can claim the prize of life. That's not what this book is about. *Yes Yes living is a way of life*, not an instant success formula that cooks in three minutes.

It begins where you *are*. Right now!

I often think about the question that was asked the conductor of a great symphony orchestra. "What instrument do you think is the most difficult to play?"

The old conductor thought for a moment, then said, "Second fiddle. I can get plenty of first violinists. But to find one who can play second fiddle with enthusiasm—that's a problem. And if we have no second fiddles, we have no harmony."

Start right now. Right where you are. Make a little harmony. The grass isn't really greener on the other side of the fence. Take a new look at your present world and realize that there are countless people who would gladly trade places with you. It's really not so bad. And you can make it so much better.

Think about Bob and Ellen Greene in Louisville who wanted to sell their home. They called a friend who was a real estate agent. He wrote an elaborate description of it and read it to them for their approval.

"Read it again," Bob said. He glanced at his wife, then leaned back in the chair and closed his eyes.

After a second reading, he was silent for a moment. Then he said thoughtfully, "I don't think we'll sell. We've been looking for that kind of place all our lives, but until you read that description, I didn't know we had it. Really, I think we'll keep the place." Ellen agreed.

The Greenes discovered what so many fail to see. *Yes Yes living begins where you are.* It transforms *you* before it changes your circumstances. That, in itself, is a miracle.

SUDDENLY IT WILL HAPPEN TO YOU

My wife, Anne, is from Great Britain and we often fly there to visit her family. And while I love England, there is one thing that still bothers me. Why do the English drive on the wrong side of the road?

Recently in London, I stepped off a curb to cross Oxford Street and did what I've done a million times. My head automatically turned to the left—and I almost lost my toes to a taxi speeding by from the right.

What a shock! And it happened again and again.

We are such creatures of habit. Our subconscious takes control so quickly and we respond like robots.

Can you imagine what happened on Easter Sunday in Atlanta when the preacher's kid changed the "Ladies" and "Men" signs on the restroom doors?

The visitors read the sign but the members didn't bother.

Well, it was a panic!

Yes, our actions become *reactions*. They become automatic, and so do our *attitudes.*

The "can't do" philosophy has poisoned society to such an extent that it has become a way of life. No No living has become the norm. The poison spreads to every area of life. And it is fatal.

The World's Greatest Excuses

A prime example of No No living is the way we make excuses on the job. Just look at the ten most common cop-outs.

1. That's the way we've always done it.
2. I didn't know you were in a hurry for it.
3. That's not my department.
4. No one told me to go ahead.
5. I'm waiting for an OK.
6. How did I know this was different?
7. That's his job, not mine.
8. Wait till the boss comes back and ask him.
9. I didn't think it was that important.
10. I forgot!

There is an epidemic of "excuseitis." And even the positive approach is not always 100 percent pure. Do you say, "Yes"? Or do you say, "Yes, but"?

An advertising executive compiled a list of phrases guaranteed to throw a wet blanket over any fire of enthusiasm. Here's the list:

"Might be better if. . . ."

"I like it—it's just that. . . ."

"See your point, but. . . ."
"Let's look at it this way."
"Our procedure is. . . ."
"Yes, but. . . ."
"No, but. . . ."
"Maybe, but. . . ."
"Let me sleep on it."
Now that is Yes-No living that reflects a lazy, leaderless personality.

"I Can and I Will"

We were not born to live No No lives. It is a *learned* behavior. It is taught to us by thousands of examples.

"The police are the bad guys." "Daddy's boss is stupid." "A little lie is OK if it doesn't hurt anyone." "Why work if you can collect unemployment?" And the list goes on.

Every time I drive through a major city I am struck by the fact that I see thousands of people who are obviously living without hope.

Oh, I've seen Calcutta. But I've also seen Chicago, and Cleveland. And the empty faces of so many tell the story. That hollow look that screams, "I've had no past. I've got no present. And there is no future." Utter despair.

But just when I think there's no way out, someone crosses my path who rose from poverty to a Ph.D., from being abandoned to being acclaimed.

Suddenly it happened! They said, "I can and I will." They saw the twinkle in the star and said, "It is mine! I can reach out and touch it."

It is important to know that just as No No living is learned, so is Yes Yes living. And this book is designed so that you can discover it for yourself. Applying the principles in these chapters is like adding fuel to the jets of a Boeing 747. It moves down the runway with increasing speed and in an instant you're airborne. And what a feeling that is.

Suddenly, it will happen to you. Like the furry caterpillar becomes a lovely butterfly, you will emerge into a new world and begin to soar in the sunlight. "For you are all sons of light and sons of day. We are not of night nor of darkness" (1 Thessalonians 5:5).

YOU CAN LIVE FOREVER

When Edwina McKenzie, ninety-one years old, was asked her secret for living a long and happy life, her reply was, "It was mainly due to getting off the *Titanic* after it hit an iceberg."

You may laugh at Edwina's reply, but someday you may be asked the same question. What will you say when they ask: "What is your secret for a long life?"

The answer given by most alert, alive, active older people is that they found *something to do*.

At sixty-three, John Wayne won his first Oscar.

Konrad Adenauer was elected chancellor of West Germany at sixty-three, and won reelection the final time at age eighty-one.

At sixty-five, Harland Sanders retired. Then he started the Kentucky Fried Chicken Corporation.

At age seventy, Golda Meir, a schoolteacher from Milwaukee, became Prime Minister of Israel.

Grandma Moses, the great American primitive painter, began her career at seventy-eight. She worked every day until she was 101.

You say, these are *exceptions*. Of course they are! *Anyone* who never gives up is an exception. And you have exactly the same potential.

After all, age is only important if you want it to be. I've seen people "washed up" at twenty-seven, and I've seen people really start to live at sixty-one. It is only our culture that puts a stigma on those in their sixties and seventies.

Perhaps we should adopt the philosophy of the Orient where they actually lie about their age—they always say they are *older*. They want to be as old as they can as *fast* as they can.

Why? Because in China and Japan *age is wisdom*. And it is!

Start Again at My Age?

Several months ago a good friend of mine asked me to meet him for a cup of coffee. I could tell something was really bothering him. It was written all over his face.

Frank talked for a while and then got to the point. "Neil," he said, "I've just turned fifty and I need some advice. I've got a real opportunity with a new company, but it just frightens me to death to start a new career at my age."

"At your age!" I responded. "Tell me, Frank. What's your future if you stay where you are?"

"Just doing what I'm doing now, till I retire."

I quizzed him about the new opportunity and he got excited. He talked about the challenge, the chance to be creative, and the potential reward.

To me the choice was simple. "Do it," I told him. "What difference does it make if you launch a new course at fifty, or twenty-eight, or seventy-two?"

I saw Frank again last week and he was still on the mountaintop. "Neil, this is the greatest experience I've ever had. I've never been happier at anything in my life."

Remember, *your age is not as important as your attitude.* And if you think like Bernard Baruch, you'll never get old. "To me," said the elder statesman, "old age is always fifteen years older than I am."

And how old are you?

Don't tell me your age. Tell me what is happening in your life.

Bert Webb, campus pastor at Evangel College in Springfield, Missouri (he took the post when he was in his seventies), has the right answer when someone asks his age. Says Webb, "I was born in nineteen and none-of-your-business."

He epitomizes Yes Yes living because he communicates on the level of college students and they love his enthusiasm. The experience has added life to his years.

"Pappy" Keeps On Living

I attended a funeral in St. Petersburg, Florida, recently. "Pappy" had passed from this life. He was in his eighties.

His friends came from several states. Pappy was

born in Georgia, moved to Detroit in the industrial revolution and retired from General Motors after more than thirty years of work.

But this was not a typical funeral. Five minutes before the service, relatives and friends were standing before the open casket and they were actually hugging one another, smiling, and even laughing out loud. It was like a celebration!

Finally someone sensed what was happening and said, "You know, Pappy would want it this way. If he could, he'd be standing right here having a good time with us."

And that's true. Pappy loved life. He always had a smile. He would go out of his way to help someone. And when his friends came to pay their last respects, they gave him their greatest gift—joy.

Pappy was my grandfather. And as far as I am concerned he will live forever. I, for one, can never forget him.

No matter what your age, remember that *you've got a lifetime ahead of you.* It may be long. It may be short. But it is a valuable lifetime that is not worth wasting on fears or tears. Stop crying and start trying!

MAKE A YES YES COMMITMENT

Why are some days "great" and others "terrible"? Is it chance? Is it luck?

No!

Good days can actually be created. Right now, you can commit yourself to an exciting Yes Yes day.

Several years ago, my friend Mel Brown asked me to

be his guest at an awards banquet of the Chase National Life Insurance Company. The speaker was to be the famed author, Napoleon Hill.

Of course, I accepted. His book, *Think and Grow Rich*, has been a great inspiration to me.

But when Hill was introduced it was obvious his age had caught up with him. We all wondered if the octogenarian would be physically able to give the speech.

He slowly walked to the podium, looked at the audience, and said something I can never forget.

Napoleon Hill said, "Ladies and Gentlemen, I have given this speech hundreds and hundreds of times in my life. But tonight I am going to deliver it the best it has ever been given. This is going to be the best speech of my life."

Wow! It was like a bolt of lightning. I watched 300 adults move to the edge of their chairs and absorb every word like a sponge.

What had happened? Why was Hill so successful? It was simply that he had committed himself to an exciting speech. He set a course of action that did not allow for failure.

You can do it, too. Just as you can talk yourself into depression, failure and fatigue, you can also speak the word to turn your day around. Yes, to turn your *life* around.

Isn't it time you had a serious talk with yourself? Isn't it time to commit yourself to Yes Yes living?

The Greatest Commitment
The most sterling example of extraordinary living

ever recorded is that of the life of Christ. In every encounter, He inspired people to live the abundant life. His objectives were clear. His words were those of one who was totally committed.

"I *will* not cast you out."

"I *will* build my church."

"I *will* be with you always."

"I *will* draw all men unto me."

"I *will* come again."

Nothing could be more affirmative. And just read of the encounters Jesus had with people and you will see that He was committed to helping in the most positive way.

Do you recall what happened when the Pharisees brought to Christ a woman caught committing adultery?

They said, "Now in the Law, Moses commanded us to stone such women; what then do You say?"

His answer startled them. He said, "He who is without sin among you, let him be the first to throw a stone at her." One by one the men left and Jesus stood alone with the woman.

He looked at her and said, "Woman, where are they? Did no one condemn you?"

"No one, Lord," she answered.

And Jesus said, "Neither do I condemn you; go your way; from now on sin no more" (John 8:3-11).

What an example! He could have berated her, but He didn't. No, He did not scorn her. He simply said, "Don't do it again!" Yes, He made a commitment that said, "I will not cast you out." But more than that, He put it into practice. He *demonstrated* His commitment.

What about your commitment? Before you read one more page it's time to make a declaration. It's time to make a Yes Yes commitment.

Go ahead and say it, *"With God's help I will begin to live the Yes Yes life."*

Here's Where It Starts

Now we can begin! You have decided to apply the principles of Yes Yes living, and that is 99 percent of the battle.

In this book you will discover:
- How to eliminate negative living.
- How to break the worry habit.
- How to develop a Yes Yes vocabulary.
- How to turn enemies into friends.
- How to live by objectives.
- How to be thankful for problems.
- How to apply the greatest commandment.
- How to turn hope into reality.
- How to develop a Yes Yes team.
- How to reach your highest goal.

But most important, you will learn to *apply* Yes Yes living to every area of your life. Every day. Every hour. Every minute. Finally, it will become a habit. You won't even think about *trying*. The change will be *total*.

Now if you *know* there are areas of your life that are trapped in the No No world and you are content to stay as you are—please give this book to someone else.

But if you are committed to a life that finds no fault, that speaks no evil, that praises rather then condemns— *read on*.

Far too many are like the art student touring a great gallery in Florence, Italy. He made critical remarks of every masterpiece he saw. The guide was getting more upset by the minute. Finally he just couldn't take it any longer. He walked up to the student and said, "Young man, these masterpieces are not on trial—*you are!*"

The concepts you are about to read have been tested. *They work.*

I am asking you to accept them, to apply them, and to adopt them as your very own.

Life itself is a miracle. And this book is about *living.* It is about *YOU!*

2

You Can Escape the No No World!

Last week while listening to my car radio I heard the weather forecast. It was "partly cloudy." Then I turned the dial to another station and the forecast was "partly sunny."

Who was right? Well, they *both* were, but what a difference in the forecast. One reporter looked for clouds and the other searched for the sun.

What would your prediction be? How do you see the world? Is it bad and getting worse, or good and getting better?

Here's how one man described the younger generation. "The children now love luxury. They have bad manners, contempt for authority, they show disrespect for their elders. They no longer rise when elders enter the room. They contradict their parents, chatter before company, gobble up food at the table, and are tyrants over their teachers."

No, that discourse wasn't made at last week's PTA

meeting. Those are the words of Socrates, the Greek philosopher. And they were given more than 300 years before Christ.

Things haven't changed. People have always looked at life from a No No point of view.

Think about what happened in London about 200 years ago when the umbrella was first seen on the streets. Religious groups went on a rampage. They tried to have the new contraption banned. And their argument was simple: "Man is interfering with heavenly design by not getting wet."

It is *natural* to resist change. It is *natural* to see the darkest cloud. It is *natural* to be trapped in the No No world.

But there is a supernatural world that offers an escape. It is a real world that can be yours.

NEGATIVES BELONG IN THE DARKROOM

Recently I was in a hurry for a photo to illustrate a story I was writing. I called my friend Chris who is an excellent photographer. He shot the picture and rushed to the darkroom.

About an hour later Chris returned. He handed me the negatives and said, "Here they are."

"I can't tell anything from these," was my response. "Where is the *positive?* I know I'm in a hurry, but negatives belong in the darkroom."

And they do!

Too often, negatives are the only pictures we see. And in many cases they are the only things we *want* to see.

Take the case of the bishop who was paying his

annual visit to a small religious college before the turn of the century. He was discussing the state of the world while visiting the home of one of the professors.

The bishop said, "Because everything about nature has been discovered and since all possible inventions have been made, the world is on the verge of the millennium."

But the prof didn't agree. He ventured that the next fifty years would produce many exciting discoveries.

"Many?" shouted the bishop. "Name just one!"

The professor said, "In the next few years man will be able to fly like the birds."

"Nonsense," laughed the bishop. "Flight is reserved for the angels."

The bishop's name was Wright. He had two sons, Orville and Wilbur.

Have things really changed? Think for a moment and you'll probably recall people who told you, "Man will never land on the moon."

You're Going to Find What You Look For

Without question, if you search for the worst you're going to discover it. "Seek and ye shall find," is not a promise of success. It is a basic truth that can work for good, or it can destroy you.

What are you looking for?

When Jason brought home his first "D" on his seventh grade report card, his dad was furious. He called his son into his study and said sternly, "What's this I see on your report card?"

Jason looked up and said, "Dad, I sure hope it's the five A's I got."

His father found exactly what he was looking for. But why begin by finding fault? Why not start by developing a positive picture?

Remember, there is always a bright side to every circumstance. There is a brilliant sun waiting behind the blackest thundercloud. *It is always shining.*

Begin right now to let that sun brighten every event of your day.

Humorist Sam Levenson knows what it means to look for the best. He is a short man, but he doesn't let it bother him. At a dinner recently, he was surrounded by a group of rather tall businessmen.

"Don't you feel quite small among these big men?" someone asked him.

"Yes I do," was Levenson's reply. "I feel like a dime among a lot of pennies."

Now that's a Yes Yes way to look at it.

Jump to the Right Conclusion

Too often we develop instant "negatives" because we start with a point of view that is predetermined. We are quick to criticize. But is our criticism justified or is it designed to detract from our own inferiority?

Let's give somebody a chance. Would we jump to the same conclusion if we were talking about a close personal friend? If we really knew the situation, would it change our behavior?

The next time you feel the urge to make a hasty judgment, think about the couple driving through North Carolina. The husband saw an old black man sitting in a chair in his garden. He was hoeing. The husband turned to his wife and said, "Now that's the height of laziness!"

But suddenly he had a lump in his throat as he saw a pair of crutches lying on the ground next to the old man's chair.

Isn't it time to develop those negatives into positive portraits of life? Look for the best and you'll certainly discover it.

HOW TO MAKE GREAT MISTAKES

Nobody's perfect!

The sooner you realize that mistakes and errors are important ingredients in life's recipe, the better off you'll be. In fact, some successful people make "mistakes on purpose" simply because it helps people know they are real.

There are two categories of mistakes: those *we* make, and the errors of others. Let's look at our own faults first.

Can you recall the last mistake you made? I certainly hope so. Because you should be making them every day. It's a sure sign of success.

Peter Drucker, whose *Peter Principle* has become renown, has some good news for people who aren't perfect.

"The better a man is the more mistakes he will make, for the more new things he will try. I would never promote into a top-level job a man who was not making mistakes, and big ones at that. Otherwise, he is sure to be mediocre. Worse still, not having made mistakes, he will not have learned how to spot them

21

early and how to correct them. And those two qualifications are among the most important for a top job."

Mistakes can also prove we are human. I know a well-known public speaker who begins his lecture by "accidentally" dropping his note cards on the floor. The audience laughs, but he is suddenly "on their level" for the rest of the speech.

Yes, errors are "OK." Start making progress and you'll start making mistakes. Remember that the No No world wants you to be a perfectionist who is "up tight" and worried about every action. But you can break free as you realize that "goofs" are great. Be thankful for them.

Instant Forgiveness!

Your personal mistakes can be positive, but what about the miscues of others?

Most mistakes are mere accidents, but do you treat them as such? The typical reaction to an error is, "Why in the world did you do that?" Or, "You did that on purpose, didn't you?"

Wait just a minute! *Stop stumbling over faults.* You can see hundreds every day and they can rob you of the very joy of life.

One of the keys to your escape from the No No world is the key of *"instant forgiveness."* Even when a mistake seems directed toward you, give an immediate response that says, "It's all right. I won't hold it against you."

Start to practice Paul's advice as he tells you to ". . . put on a heart of compassion . . . forgiving each other . . . just as the Lord forgave you, so also should you" (Colossians 3:12, 13).✦

If there is anger—Forgive!

If there is resentment—Forgive!

If there is bitterness—Forgive!

Hear the echo from the cross. "Father forgive them, for they know not what they do."

Millions have granted pardon and you can do it too. What a feeling of freedom to wipe the slate clean! To perform an act of grace! To instantly forgive!

When I look at the engraving on a penny I think about Abe Lincoln's second inaugural address when he said, "With malice toward none, with charity for all."

Put Pardon Into Practice

Sure, we're going to stumble, bungle, trip, and even fall. But so are our friends. We're all in this thing together.

What happened in Des Moines is a good example. The tennis courts of a local high school are right next to the beautiful grounds of a church. And every once in a while a ball flies over the fence and lands on the manicured lawn.

Recently, a player chasing a ball came face to face with a large sign that read "NO TRESPASSING." But the sign came down when the students put up their own sign on the fence facing the church. It read, "FORGIVE US OUR TRESPASSES."

The "No" became a "Yes" and both the students and the church were better for it.

Mistakes? Forgive them and forget them. Even when the blunders are your own and you feel the laughter and ridicule of others, just keep moving straight ahead.

Remember that opposition is necessary.

Even a small fire begins to roar when it is disturbed.

Thank God for every conflict, every error, and every chance to forgive.

TURN YOUR MINUS INTO A PLUS

In the first grade you learned to add and to subtract. Unfortunately, most people apply the "minus sign" to more than math. It is applied to attitude, self-image, personal relationships, and it affects our entire personality.

Again, we become victims of the No No world. But the minus can be turned to a plus.

Here's how it worked for a businessman.

In the window of a locksmith's shop was a sign: "Keys Made While You Wait." Business was slow and he tried to figure out what the problem was.

He finally decided that people just don't like to wait. So he changed the sign to read: "Keys Made While You Watch."

It was magic. His sales zoomed and the business was transformed almost overnight. Instead of "waiting," people were "watching."

Think of the difference just one word makes.

When you stop to think about it, it is easier to change a minus (–) into a plus (+) than to erase part of the plus. All it takes is adding a vertical line and there it is.

It's like adding an exclamation point!

But the real excitement starts when you look for opportunities to demonstrate it.

The Volkswagen That Climbed Stairs

The next time you are faced with a "minus" situation, take a "plus" action. Here's how John Wilson did it when he was dean of students at a ministerial training school.

John was awakened in the middle of the night by a knock on his apartment door which was just off the lobby of the men's dormitory.

He opened the door, looked into the lobby and couldn't believe his eyes. There was his little Volkswagen! It had been carried up a flight of stairs and placed right in front of his door.

Wilson's natural reaction would have been to wake up the residence hall, find the culprits, and dish out the punishment.

But what did he do? He walked around the VW and laughed out loud. And when the strong-armed pranksters peeked around the corner and saw his surprising behavior, they actually became proud of their feat and said, "Hey! Can you believe we actually did it?"

John said, "You know, this is really amazing. I've got to see how you did it. I'll bet you can't carry this thing back down those stairs."

"Just watch us," was the reply. And that was the end of the prank.

Can you imagine what could have happened if he had punished the criminals? Well, he would have been tormented by pranks the rest of the semester.

Right now, try this simple mental exercise. Think of a situation you would describe as horrible. It may involve problems of finances, people, or even your physical well-being. Then, remembering how John Wilson solved his VW crisis, think of the best possible solution to your make-believe problem.

Yes, if you stop to think about it, there is always a "plus" in the picture.

Follow the Farmer's Example

The No No world has convinced people they must be *against* more than they are *for*. But don't accept that lie.

When someone asks your opinion, *state what you are for.*

In Washington I heard about a fellow who stopped to watch a farmer spraying his apple trees to prevent codling moth damage to the apples.

The man walked up to the farmer and asked, "How come you're so dead set against the codling moth?"

The farmer's reply surprised him. "I'm not really *against* the codling moth, but I sure am *for* apples."

Let me ask, *"What are you for?"*

The world is searching for people who are *for* something. People who can turn that minus into a plus. People who put it into practice and see exciting possibilities begin to unfold.

Here's what happened to Carol Barton in St. Louis.

Carol applied for the position of assistant office manager of a large insurance firm. She was given an extremely lengthy application form to complete.

On the last page was a box space reserved for the employing official to fill in a confidential evaluation and the amount of salary to be paid. Above the box were the words: "DO NOT WRITE IN THIS SPACE."

But Carol had a positive sense of humor and wrote these words in the box: "DO RIGHT IN THIS SPACE."

She got the job.

Like flipping a coin, you can turn "tails" into "heads." Yes, it's possible to transform "shouldn't," "can't," and "won't" into "should," "can," and "will."

It's all up to you!

THE GREATEST PLACE IN THE WORLD

In a sociology class at Ohio State, Dr. Wallace asked us to make a list of ten successful people we had met. Then he asked us to discuss the common denominators of these people.

Did they have rich parents?

Were they good looking?

Did they have an outstanding education?

For the rest of the class period we mixed and matched our lists until one common cord seemed to hold the group together.

More than 90 percent of those we listed had lived in their own town for the past fifteen years. And most of them much longer.

There it was. Plain and simple. *Success was directly linked with stability.*

Right Where You Are

Escaping the No No world isn't always accomplished by calling the Mayflower Moving Company. The skies aren't always bluer on the other side of the continent.

Instead, try this. Take a fresh look at your immediate surroundings and you'll see incredible possibilities. Right where you live there are some of the happiest people in the world who wouldn't trade places with a king.

You can be among them. In fact, you already *are* among them.

Now if you were to list your favorite places would you include Bismark, North Dakota or Needles, California?

Well, I've been to Bismark and the folks I met think it's the greatest spot on the globe. One fellow told me, "We really love it, especially in January and February. Our winters are fantastic."

Bismark is filled with successful people who have built their lives and their fortunes there. They love the place because they love their friends, their work, their church, and their *stability*.

I've also talked with a real estate broker in Needles, California. The town is so hot in July that you can fry an egg on the sidewalk at midnight. But he said, "Say, this place is about as close to heaven as you can get."

Actually, I had another place in mind.

For some funny reason it caused me to recall a cartoon I saw as a boy. Two ugly apes were kissing each other. The caption read, "What you like depends on what you are used to."

But some people never get used to anything—except moving. They are ready to relocate at the drop of a hat, and they will drop the hat!

Where is the greatest place in the world? Right here! Right where you are.

Build your life on a strong foundation.

Right where you are.

Surround yourself with lifelong friends.

Right where you are.

Get involved in building a community.

Right where you are.

Let your roots grow deep. Watch your life stand tall.

Right where you are.

The Good Life in New Hope

On the other side of the globe I saw what can happen when people decide to make the best out of the worst possible circumstance. It was in Liberia, in West Africa, and I'll never forget it.

Two native guides, who had adopted the names Moses and Samson, placed our luggage on their heads and we began the twelve-hour walk from Fellika to New Hope Town.

My father and I were walking through some of the most dense jungle you can imagine. Our goal was the leper colony called New Hope.

It would take a chapter to describe the events of that one day. We sloshed through streams, were frightened by snakes, and our feet were swollen with blisters as we limped into the colony.

But our pain was absolutely nothing compared to

what we saw.

Lepers without limbs. Faces distorted by flesh that had fallen away. Open "ulcers" being treated by mission nurses.

It was not a beautiful sight.

The next morning, however, my life was touched as I saw that the lepers were not alone. Their entire families were with them. It was "home." This was their life.

Each day they gathered in the chapel to sing and to pray. I can still see their radiant faces as they sang, "I've Got Joy Like a River." And I will not forget the leper who prayed, "Thank you, Lord, for bringing me to this place. Thank you, Lord, for allowing me to live with all of these beautiful people."

The colony certainly had the right name. It was a town of New Hope. And it made the words of Paul come to life as he states: "I have learned to be content in whatever circumstances I am" (Philippians 4:11).

The Keys to Your Escape

The great escape from the No No world is not a trick of Houdini. Instead, it is a planned, positive approach to life itself.

As we have seen, the keys to your escape include:

1. Your ability to look for the best.
2. Your ability to forgive.
3. Your ability to turn a minus into a plus.
4. Your ability to see the possibilities in your present circumstances.

Yes, you already have the ability. Start putting it

into practice.

Unfortunately, some people attempt to be "pro" and "con" at the same time. But it just won't work.

When he wrote his second letter to the church at Corinth, Paul talked about the problem. He asked: "When I make my plans, do I make them from selfish motives, ready to say 'Yes, yes' and 'No, no' at the same time?" (2 Corinthians 1:17 TEV).

Then he gave the answer that presents the source of Yes Yes living. "As God is true, my promise to you was not a 'Yes' and a 'No.' For Jesus Christ the Son of God . . . is not one who is 'Yes' and 'No.' On the contrary, he is God's 'Yes'; for it is he who is the 'Yes' to all of God's promises" (2 Corinthians 1:18-20 TEV).

It's exciting to know that we are not on our own as we begin the Yes Yes life.

What a promise!

3

Consider the Possibilities!

A friend told me about a mother who was having a hard time getting her son to go to school one morning.

"Nobody likes me at school," said the son.

"The teachers don't and the kids don't. The superintendent wants to transfer me, the bus drivers hate me, the school board wants me to drop out, and the custodians have it in for me. I don't want to go."

"You've *got* to go," insisted the mother.

"You're healthy. You have a lot to learn. You've got something to offer. You are a leader. Besides, you are forty-nine years old. And you are the principal."

How true! And I'm sure that more than a school administrator can identify with the situation.

We have been caught up in a world of fear, anxiety, and worry.

Our fear destroys our confidence.

Our anxiety destroys our health.

Our worry destroys our will to succeed.

Franklin Delano Roosevelt was absolutely right when he said, "The only thing we have to fear is fear itself." It was true after the Great Depression. It is true today.

Can you say farewell to fear? I'm certain that you can. Let's consider the possibilities.

IS IT WORTH THE WORRY?

A recent national Harris poll asked Americans to tell what worried them the most. More than half the sample worried about:

- Wasting too much time.
- Not learning enough.
- Eating too much.
- Being out of shape physically.

If you were asked to prepare such a list, what would it include? Job security? The future of your family? Inflation? The possibility of war?

There are millions of people who have legitimate fears of unemployment, hunger, or violence. But there are millions more who live in an affluent society who are dying of worry.

Yes, *worry is a killer*. People are dying from it every day.

Mental Strangulation

The next time you find yourself bound by extraordinary worry, stop to consider what is really happening to you.

The word "worry" itself comes from the old German word *wurgen*, which means "to choke." Then, through the years, the term came to be used to denote "mental strangulation."

It's true. There is a clear connection between the physical act of strangling and the mental process of worrying. And the longer you dwell on your fears, your cares, your anxieties, the more your body begins to "choke."

You question, "Will it really kill me?"

Listen to the founder of the Mayo Clinic, Dr. Charles H. Mayo: "Worry affects the circulation, the heart, the glands, the whole nervous system. I have never known a man who died from overwork, but many who have died of doubt."

Last summer while walking down a street in the heart of Baltimore, I saw a small sign in the window of an insurance agency. I'll never forget its powerful statement.

The sign read: *"Cancer is curable, but the fear of cancer is fatal."*

No doubt about it. Your body is drastically affected by fear and worry. That's why the concepts in this book are so important.

You are being asked to replace fear with faith. To replace worry with the will to win.

How can it be done?

First you need to realize that *most of your fears never materialize.* In nearly every case, your worry is simply not necessary.

Why Worry?

Take the case of the medical doctor in Boston who

became furious about a newspaper article that criticized his personal life. He became convinced that his character had been defamed. It was all he could think about and it was destroying his life.

His next-door neighbor was a counselor at Boston University and he sought his advice.

"Tell me. What should I do about it?"

"Absolutely nothing," said the neighbor.

"Half the people who got the paper didn't read the story. Half who read it didn't understand it. Half who did understand it didn't believe it. And half of those who believed it are of no importance anyway."

So why worry? It's really not worth it.

Next, you need to consider that *life goes on whether you worry or not.*

We all have friends who are classic "worry warts." I have one, too.

The last time he shared his current list of "life and death" concerns I interrupted with a question. "Tell me, Tom. What were you worrying about one year ago at this time? How about two years ago? Or three?"

He was stunned by his own answer.

"You know, I can't even remember what was bothering me six months ago."

Worry is like any type of addiction. It starts as a small concern, but becomes a giant habit that hooks us. It becomes bigger than life. It surrounds us and swallows us.

It reminds me of fog.

The U.S. Bureau of Standards says that dense fog covering seven city blocks 100 feet deep is composed of something less than one eight-ounce glass of water. It is divided into more than 60 thousand million drops.

It sounds impossible, but one glass of water can shut down O'Hare International Airport and can completely affect our ability to see.

Your worry has the same power. One tiny trouble, if allowed to multiply, can cloud your entire life. And you'll lose your vision.

Let the sunshine in. Let the brightness of Yes Yes living evaporate those clouds of doubt.

It's up to you.

A NEW LOOK AT LIFE

Bournemouth, England, is one of the most beautiful spots in Great Britain. Hundreds of thousands flock to its beaches every summer.

My wife and I decided to accept the invitation of relatives to spend a few days at this famous seaside resort.

But July in Britain is not like July in the United States. The weather can be anything from mild to cloudy and cold.

You guessed it. It was cold. We didn't see the sun for days.

Each morning we would bundle up and take a long walk along the beach to the pier at Bascombe.

To my amazement, in that cold, misty weather, there were hundreds of people on the beach. They were in swimsuits and having a fantastic time playing soccer, building sandcastles, and splashing in the waves.

I asked my British friends how they braved the cold

and their answer surprised me.

"You see, we only have two weeks for vacation and we've booked our holiday long in advance. If the sun does not shine it does not shine. But we are going to have a jolly good time anyway."

That was it! They made a decision to have a great vacation—no matter what the weather.

It gave me a new perspective on life.

When it rains on my picnic, I think about the British.

When my plane is canceled and I'm stranded in Evansville, I think about the British.

When my best laid plans don't materialize, I think about the British.

If they can smile while others shiver, so can I. And *so can you!*

It's All in How You See It

Take a new look at life.

Sure, there are thousands of things that can go wrong. And, according to Murphy's Law, they probably will.

But are you going to let life's disappointments rob you of your right to smile? Let's hope not.

Instead, decide in advance that no matter what happens you are going to take it in stride. You are going to enjoy life to its fullest.

Charles Vincent has a great reputation on Wall Street. Every morning his chauffeur drives him from his beautiful home near Darien, Connecticut, to Manhattan.

One morning Vincent's driver was standing in front

of his limousine and a stranger came up and asked: "Oh, you work for Mr. Vincent?"

The chauffeur threw his shoulders back and said, "I beg your pardon. Certainly not. Mr. Vincent works for me."

"How's that?" the stranger asked.

"He gets up at six o'clock every morning and comes down to this filthy stinking city to make enough money to keep me and this Cadillac going!"

Now that's a new way to look at things. The chauffeur decided to view life from a new vantage point, and his own value was increased.

Your worth can multiply, too.

It has been said that, "All wealth is intelligence applied to raw materials."

When you pause to think about it, the piece of paper bearing George Washington's signature was worth only a half a penny. But it was sold at an auction for several thousands of dollars.

Less than two feet of canvas worth just a few French francs became valued at over $200,000 because Renoir applied his great talent to the white cloth.

The same principle applies today.

What's Your Real Value?

Several years ago I was having dinner at the home of a printer. He was talking about his business when he made a unique observation.

"Neil, every day I print items for customers that are sold for ten and twenty times the cost of the paper. I sure wish I could come up with my own product that would earn that kind of profit for me."

Right on the spot we had a brainstorming session that resulted in the formation of a publishing company called Mid-America Research.

We formed a partnership that was simple. I would write the material and he would print at cost. We would split the profits.

We decided to publish research material for high-school and college debate teams. It was an immediate success. Thousands of orders came in through a direct-mail campaign.

Several years later I sold my half of the business for a sizable amount.

The company found a needed product that could be printed on inexpensive paper and sold at a profit.

But the greatest raw material is not paper or cloth. It is *you!* And when inspired intelligence is applied, there is no limit to what that raw material will become.

Thinking, however, is a lost art for millions. And some folk will believe just about anything. They even accept the sign in the loan company window that reads, "Now you can borrow enough money to get completely out of debt."

But there's another way to escape debt.

You are worth much more than you can imagine. Just as the same 2½" x 6" piece of paper becomes either a one-dollar bill or a $100-bill, you need to raise the value of your stock.

Yes you can! It starts to happen when you begin to take charge of your life.

WHO'S IN CHARGE HERE?

I always enjoy reading the "before" and "after" ads in national magazines. It's no accident that the Madison Avenue photographer makes certain the "before" model is either frowning or expressing pain. Then along comes the solution. An aspirin. Sunburn relief. A new laundry detergent. Presto, there's one of the brightest faces you can imagine.

It happens in real life, too. As you begin to act on the possibilities of Yes Yes living, you start to distinguish between the "old you" and the "new you."

There's an old Hindu proverb that says, "There is nothing noble in being superior to some other man. The true nobility is being superior to your previous self."

I certainly don't buy reincarnation, but that statement is absolutely right.

So often we trudge through life with a goal "to be better than the next guy." It starts in school as we take tests to learn how we compare with others in the first grade.

But the real question is this: *How far have you come since you last took the test?* In other words, how are you doing *personally*? Are you really superior to your previous self?

The Measuring Stick

The most dramatic "then" and "now" commercial you'll ever see will be your own story. It will happen when you call a truce in your battle with your boss, your family, or your business competition. *Because the real war must be waged on the inside.*

41

The final victory will be won as the "new you" is declared the winner.

Dwight L. Moody, the great evangelist, liked to tell his audience, "I have more trouble with myself than with any other man I have ever met."

It's true of you, too. And the sooner you admit it and act upon it, the faster your progress will be.

At the Great Judgment, will you be asked, "Well, let's see, how did you compare with that fellow Bill, or Jerry?"

It won't be how you *compare*. It's how you *measure up* to God's Word. And that's the big difference.

Start today to set some objectives and to establish some "progress points." *Know where you are* and it will be easy to see how far you have come.

Reaching your goal requires more than a casual effort. It takes clear goals plus hard work.

When basketball coach Gene Smithson came to the campus of Wichita State, he changed the team's image from dull to dynamite.

During his first season there were signs in the Henry Levitt Arena and all over town with the letters "MTXE."

What did it mean? The fans soon learned that those letters represented Smithson's philosophy of coaching. "Mental Toughness—Extra Effort."

Says the coach, "I firmly believe in mental toughness and extra effort for players on my team. We expect much from ourselves and from the players."

It works off the basketball court, too.

Following a speaking engagement for a medical association in Sarasota, Florida, a fellow came up and asked if he could speak to me privately. He was a doctor.

That night I had given my lecture, "The Miracle of Total Commitment."

The man said, "I just wanted you to know that I made a personal resolution tonight. I've been smoking four packs of cigarettes a day and I made a decision to quit as of right now."

"Great!" I said. "Here's my card. Drop me a note in a month or so. Let me know what happens."

More than one year later, after I had completely forgotten the incident, I received a letter from the physician.

The paragraph that caught my attention said, "Quiting smoking that night was really one of the easiest things I've ever done. I had tried many times before but it was all in my head and it just didn't work. But that night it was a total decision of my mind, my mouth, my hands, just every part of me. And that was it!"

Well, here's what happened to the doctor.

He conquered his habit by conquering himself. It was total! And it will work for you as well.

Conquer yourself and eliminate worry.

Conquer yourself and increase self-worth.

Conquer yourself and take charge of your future.

Conquer yourself and give that extra effort.

When you win the skirmish with self, you've really won the war.

THE BLIND CAN REALLY SEE!

Some time ago, while on a speaking tour of high schools in the Northeast, I was scheduled to speak to the students at the State School for the Blind in Batavia, New York.

That year I was presenting a program on world affairs based on my experiences traveling in Africa. To illustrate the program I used several artifacts.

But what should I do at the school for the blind? Should I just talk? What possible benefit would the visual material be?

Well, I decided to present the program just as I would to any other audience. But at the end of my talk I invited the students to the front to "feel" some of the articles I was referring to.

A young lady about thirteen years old stood before the table and asked, "May I look at the carved elephant tusk you talked about?"

I thought it strange that she would ask to "look" at something she could not see.

But I was even more surprised when she held it and exclaimed, "Oh! This is really beautiful. It's the most beautiful carving I've ever seen."

At that moment I realized that she had a power of sight far greater than my own. She was not seeing with her eyes. She was seeing with her fingers, with her mind, with her *heart*.

Your Head or Your Heart

What a beautiful world it is when your heart gets involved.

In education, there is a clear distinction made between *thinking* and *feeling*. The *cognitive domain* involves the mind. What do we mean? How do we com-

44

prehend? How do we analyze it? How do we apply it?

But there's another world known as the *affective domain* that involves the heart. How do you feel about it? What about your emotions? What have you experienced?

Your life won't change at all if Yes Yes living stops at the cognitive level. The only benefit will be your ability to explain the basics of Yes Yes living to someone else.

But if that's the only benefit, you'd be better off spending your time with an encyclopedia.

Oh, there's so much more. And you'll recognize the drastic change once you decide to allow the principles of this book to enter the *affective* domain of your life.

You'll *feel* the joy of positive living.

You'll *experience* the thrill of a new outlook on life.

Yes Yes living will flow from your heart.

Like the blind girl in Batavia, you'll know what it's like to really see.

The Inside Story

Last night while looking through my wife's *Ladies Home Journal,* I saw dozens of ads offering help for the *exterior.* The ads read:

"She conked out but her hair held up!"

"Me gray? No way!"

"Don't gamble with your teeth!"

But there was little relief for the inside (unless you include, "When it's more than a headache, send for Sine-Off!").

We are caught up in an age of cosmetic surgery that

seems to ignore the fact that it is what's on the inside that counts.

George Bernard Shaw was talking about more than the surface when he said: "Better keep yourself clean and bright; you are the window through which you must see the world."

Think about it! A well-scrubbed heart lifts the smog from our vision. Clean thinking and clean living go hand in hand.

Once I heard a motivational speaker say, "You know what the Good Book says about. . . . 'As a man thinketh, so is he.'"

Whoa! That's not what it says at all. You've got to add the three missing words. "For as he thinketh in his heart, so is he" (Proverbs 23:7 KJV). Where? *In his heart!*

Real living flows from the heart, not from the head. And that is the source of your thought life, too.

Even your speech is a reflection of *the real you.* "For the mouth speaks out of that which fills the heart" (Matthew 12:34).

Simply trying to think good thoughts and speak clever words won't produce Yes Yes living. Your true character is revealed by what is on the inside. And that is why it is so important to make sure your heart is crystal clear and bright.

Here's some great advice from the Book of Proverbs: "Watch over your heart with all diligence, for from it flows the springs of life" (Proverbs 4:23).

Is This the Real You?

Once there was a man who built a financial empire

through a positive-thinking sales force. His followers drove cars they couldn't afford. They wore the best clothes and jewelry.

His favorite phrase was, "Fake it till you make it."

Well, it didn't work. His kingdom collapsed and his followers were left owing payments on their Cadillacs.

Faking it just won't do. Yes Yes living must become part of the *true you*.

Yes, you can say goodbye to worry.

Yes, you can rise above your critics.

Yes, you can take a new look at life.

Yes, you can increase your self-worth.

Yes, you can take charge of your life.

Yes, you can conquer yourself.

And you can experience Yes Yes living as it flows from your heart.

Consider the possibilities!

4

Why Say No
When You Can Say Yes?

Is it possible that just one word can make the difference between failure and success?

That's what Bob Evans claims.

"Years ago," says Evans, "when I'd hear a statement with which I would disagree, I used to say 'Baloney!' and people began avoiding me like the plague."

"Now I substitute 'Amazing!' for 'Baloney!' and my phone keeps ringing and my list of friends continues to grow."

Your vocabulary may not be filled with "Baloney," but what you say does make a difference. Like it or not, you are judged by your conversation.

The way you listen.

The words you choose.

The interest you express in others.

And the emotion you express.

Yes, you are immediately given the "thumbs up" or "thumbs down" treatment because of both your spoken and unspoken words. That's why it is vital to develop a Yes Yes vocabulary that reflects your positive personality.

There are some specific things you can do to strengthen your powers of communication.

ARE YOU REALLY LISTENING?

The biggest problem with most conversations is that *nobody is listening*.

While Bob is talking, Mary is thinking about what she'll say.

While Mary is talking, Bob is planning his next phrase.

As a result, Bob and Mary are doing a lot of thinking, but neither one is listening. Their conversation is like two trains on separate tracks, passing in the night.

Bob knows what he wants to say. Mary, too, has something to communicate. But their objectives are in opposite directions.

Think about your own conversation. Is it one-sided? Or is there real communication taking place?

It reminds me of the speech teacher who stood in the receiving line of the Heart Fund recognition banquet. She was tired of shaking all those hands, saying, "How are you?" and hearing the same old responses.

So she thought she'd try an experiment.

She greeted the next twenty patrons in the line by smiling and quietly saying, "I have leprosy."

The responses were just incredible!

They smiled back and said things like, "How happy I

am for you," and "How wonderful. You must tell me all about it."

Only one person said, "That's the craziest thing I've ever heard." And they both stood there and laughed.

Who's Doing the Talking?

The quickest way to make a friend is to start asking questions. People love to talk and you'll be loved for listening.

Today, try to analyze your conversation. Who does most of the talking? Is it you?

Recently, I took a trip overseas that was mentioned in a local paper. That same day my telephone rang and a lady asked if she could come to my office. She wanted to talk about my trip. Of course, I was delighted.

After we shook hands, she said, "Tell me about your trip."

But as I opened my mouth, she began telling me about hers. For two hours I was saying, "Isn't that interesting!" and "How about that!" I really didn't tell her a thing.

Finally, she looked at her watch and said, "My! I've got to go. But let me tell you that you are the most interesting person I've ever talked to."

It has been said many times that "God gave us two ears and one mouth so that we could listen twice as much as we talk."

Try putting it into practice today. Seek someone out and ask them a question.

People want to tell you about their families, their friends, their hobbies, and even their illnesses. All they ask is for you to listen.

Let's face it. *We always learn more by listening than by talking*. And think of the friends we can make.

I'll never forget a sign hanging on the wall of a little restaurant in Louisville. It read, "A fish is only hooked when his mouth is open."

What is the purpose of your conversation? Is it to learn or is it to brag? Is it to build friendship or is it to build your ego?

You're at the Head Table

Self-promotion is nothing new. Sometimes we do it with our words; sometimes with our actions.

Do you recall the story in the New Testament involving the folks who attended the great wedding feast?

Jesus was conversing with the invited guests when He began to notice how they had been picking out the places of honor at the head table.

He thought some practical advice would be in order and here is what Christ said:

"When you are invited by someone to a wedding feast, do not take the place of honor, lest someone more distinguished than you may have been invited by him, and he who invited you both shall come and say to you, 'Give place to this man,' and then in disgrace you proceed to occupy the last place.

"But when you are invited, go and recline at the last place, so that when the one who has invited you comes, he may say to you, 'Friend, move up higher'; then you will have honor in the sight of all who are at the table with you.

"For everyone who exalts himself shall be humbled, and he who humbles himself shall be exalted" (Luke 14:8-11).

Yes, *the best way to "move up higher" is to let others do it for you.*

If you want honor—try humility.

If you want respect—try listening.

It really works!

WINNING THE WAR OF WORDS

It's no wonder that we have millions of people with negative vocabularies. After all, before we learned to talk, we lived in a No No world.

"No, No! Don't touch the mirror!"

"No, No! Don't put that in your mouth!"

"No, No! Don't play with the drapes!"

Somehow you survived! But what about your words? It's one thing to say "No No" to a child, but something altogether different when speaking to your peers.

It's not what you say, it's how you say it that counts.

An ancient Chinese story tells the account of a noble sultan who called in one of his seers.

"Tell me," asked the sultan, "how long will I live?"

The prophet answered bluntly, "Sire, you will live to see all your sons dead."

The sultan immediately flew into a rage, called in his guards, and ordered the execution of the prophet.

Then he asked for a second seer, who said, "Sire, I see you blessed with a long life. So long that you will outlive all your family."

Well, the old sultan was delighted. He rewarded the

seer with precious jewels and gifts.

Both prophets had the same message, but what a difference in the way they said it.

Who's Right? Who's Wrong?

Every day we are transmitting dozens of messages. Some are for punishment. But *all* can be positive.

Regardless of the circumstances, your words can have a Yes Yes ring about them.

Even when someone disagrees with you, there is little to be gained by argument. It only digs the trenches deeper and usually results in a "no win" stalemate.

Benjamin Franklin had a creative method of getting people to agree with his point of view.

He would state his case and then scratch his head and say, "That is the way it seems to me, but, of course, I may be mistaken about it."

Immediately, his listener would receive what he had to say and seeing Franklin's doubt, would try to *convince* him of it.

What a way to win an argument without a struggle! Try it.

But as long as you live you'll meet people who will disagree with you. Is it because they don't like you? Is it because they despise your logic?

No!

People usually take an opposing view simply because it makes for more interesting conversation. You probably do it every day without giving it a second thought. I'm guilty too.

But the tragedy lies in the fact that if the conversation becomes heated, a person can defend a position he really doesn't believe. But to save face, he will espouse the idea for life.

What a shame! Let's hope that you don't fall into that trap.

It's difficult to know who is right and who is wrong in an argument. I had a teacher in college who gave some advice I won't forget. She said, "If you want to know who is wrong in an argument, see who gets angry first."

Turn Down the Volume

Can you remember the last time someone shouted at you? What was your reaction?

For most people, when you are shouted at, you *shout back*. And there is only one proven method to keep someone from "hollering" during a disagreement. *Keep your voice low!* It will almost always act to control the voice of the other person.

Of course, we don't necessarily need audible words to have an argument. Even the deaf can reveal their temper.

There's a story I've told to audiences to illustrate the point. It's about two deaf mutes, a man and his wife, who were on the front porch of their home making signs at each other.

The lady was working two of her fingers up and down just like a pair of scissors. The man was moving his arms like he was swimming.

There were two fellows standing on the sidewalk

who became quite interested in the actions of the mute couple. One of the men knew a little bit of sign language and his friend asked, "What are they saying?"

The friend said, "She is telling him to go cut the lawn and he's telling her to go jump in the river."

I never found out who won the argument.

It's a sure sign, however, that you're taking control of your life when you can control your anger. As it is said: *"The more hot arguments you win, the fewer warm friends you'll have."*

The advice of Scripture is worth heeding: "A gentle answer turns away wrath, but a harsh word stirs up anger" (Proverbs 15:1, 2).

Remember, it's not what you say, it's how you say it.

TELL IT LIKE IT IS

Some people can talk about anything, but they don't know when to quit.

A speaker was asked to prepare a one-hour speech for a convention. Then, a few minutes later, he had a call that asked, "Can you cut it to thirty minutes?" The next day the program coordinator called and said, "It looks like you'll have to cut it to fifteen minutes."

He was about to be introduced to the audience when the master of ceremonies whispered in his ear, "We need you to limit your remarks to five minutes."

"Five minutes!" he retorted. "I don't understand the subject that well."

Whether you are speaking to thousands or speaking to one, you need to get to the point and keep it simple.

What Do You Mean?

Recently I was a guest on a nighttime talk show on WBZ-TV, the NBC station in Boston. It was a question-answer format with a live audience in the studio.

At one point, a young man in the audience asked a two-minute question that sailed over the heads of everyone.

Dr. Gordon Fee, who was also on the program, turned to me and whispered, "He must be a seminarian. Only a theology student could ask a totally unintelligent question like that."

Is your language simple? Is it clear? Do people really understand what you are saying?

Every time I hear someone say, "She's as pretty as she can be," I laugh. What does it mean? Is she really pretty? Or is there a limit to how pretty she could be?

It's like a review of one of my lectures written by an administrator at North Dakota State University. It read, "I cannot recommend Mr. Eskelin too highly."

Now, what did he mean by that?

We've already talked about the folly of self-promotion, but there are times we need to *tell it like it is*.

Yes Yes speaking requires a positive, direct approach.

That's the style used by Notre Dame's star center, Frankie Szymanski, when he appeared in a South Bend court as a witness in a civil suit.

"Are you a member of the Fighting Irish football team this year?" asked the judge.

"Yes, Your Honor."

"What position?"

"Center, Your Honor."

"How good a center?"

Szymanski squirmed in his chair and then said in a confident tone, "Sir, I'm the best center Notre Dame ever had."

Coach Frank Leahy was in the courtroom. He was shocked because his player had always been modest and unassuming. So after the court was adjourned, the coach asked him why he had made such a statement.

Szymanski's face turned a little red. "I hated to do it, coach," he said, "but after all, I was under oath."

He certainly told it like it was.

Try Name Calling

There is something else you can do to get a Yes Yes response from those you deal with.

Many of the world's most successful people have a habit worth copying. They call people by their names.

Of all the words in the world, there is one that has almost magical power. It can arrest your attention. It can break your most stubborn defenses. It is a special sound you never tire of.

What is that word? *Your name.*

In a recent study, people were handed a new pen to try. Ninety-seven out of a hundred wrote their own name.

A few weeks ago I was having difficulty reaching an important media executive in Los Angeles. The secretary simply would not let me talk to him. So after two calls I asked, "By the way, what is your name?"

"Judy," she said.

The next day I called again and said, "Hi! Is this Judy? How are things in L.A.?" Her response was as warm as the California sun.

Then I asked to speak to her boss. And within seconds he was on the line.

Her name seemed to make the difference. In fact, the most important word in her world was "Judy."

You say, "But I have a hard time remembering names."

Well, there are dozens of formulas designed to help you remember, but the secret of memory is this: You must *want* to remember.

We store things in our memory by design. And we forget almost everything else.

Today, learn a name. Use it. Remember it. *Call someone by his name.* It works wonders.

And while we're on the topic, what about *your* name? It's yours. So go ahead and use it.

At a seminar sponsored by Bell Telephone, the speaker made a statement that stuck with me. "Successful people," he said, "answer the phone by giving their own names."

Since that time, I have almost always answered my calls with, "Hello. This is Neil Eskelin."

Your words are your calling card. They reflect your personality and are sounds by which you are judged.

Make your words count. Make them solid. Make them firm. Let people know exactly where you stand.

James put it this way: ". . . let your yes be yes, and

your no, no" (James 5:12).

Go ahead. Tell it like it is.

SAY IT WITH A SMILE

You don't have to raise your voice, stomp your foot, or lose your temper to get your point across.

But I heard about a high-school teacher with a sense of humor who tried it.

He walked into his class one April morning and found that bedlam had broken loose. He slapped his hand on the desk, raised his voice and shouted, "I demand pandemonium!"

Immediately the class was hushed. You would have thought he had demanded quiet.

When they realized what he said, they laughed. But they got the point.

Your words aren't what they seem. It's what's behind them that determines communication.

Take the word "Yes" itself. Now the word is defined as positive, but it isn't always used that way.

"Yes" can say "I love you." But when said with a set jaw and narrowed eyes, it can mean "I hate you."

It's true that people are affected much more by the tone of your voice and the look on your face than by any selected set of words.

Recently, a prominent network television reporter was accused of "eyebrow editorializing." His words could never be held against him. But, oh, the look on his face.

On the other hand, the most unpleasant words, if said with a smile, will be accepted as positive.

If you've ever raised a child, you know the importance of Yes Yes communication.

When your kid needs correction, you have two choices. You can scold, threaten or command him; or you can use the affirmative approach.

Humpty Dumpty Sat on a Wall

I remember the night in Miami when our son, Ian, was just five years old. We were staying with relatives and it was his bedtime.

But when I looked at the living room floor, I knew we had a problem. Toys were scattered all over the place.

"Ian," I said, "you need to pick up all those toys before you go to bed."

"Daddy," he said, "I'm too tired to pick up my toys."

My immediate inclination was to force him to clean up the room. But, like Ford, I had a better idea.

Instead, I went into the bedroom, laid down, and said, "Ian, come here. Let's play Humpty Dumpty."

He climbed up on my knees and I said, "Humpty Dumpty sat on a wall. Humpty Dumpty had a great fall." And he fell.

Ian laughed and said, "Let's do it again." And again.

After each fall, he'd say, "Let's do it again."

Well, after the third "fall," I said, "Okay, but first go pick up those toys."

Without thinking, he ran into the front room and in ninety seconds he finished a job that could have taken half an hour.

Then he jumped back on my knees and repeated,

"Daddy, let's do it again."

"Ian, I thought you were too tired to pick up those toys."

"I was, daddy, but I just wanted to do *this*."

What a lesson it was for me!

Ian found the energy for something he was "too tired" to do.

Was he forced to do it? No.

Was he threatened? No.

Was he embarrassed in front of other people? No.

He cleaned up the room because *he found something he wanted to do*. And he was involved with something he enjoyed.

By the way—it was fun for me, too.

When you "say it with a smile," your ability to motivate and inspire people is multiplied.

It has been said that Scripture does not record that Christ ever smiled or laughed. And many view him as a sullen, somber figure.

But it is written that "the children gathered around him," and he "took them up in his arms." Have you ever seen children crowd around anyone who didn't smile?

Of course not.

Why not add a smile to your speech today?

What Do You Say?

Yes, you do have a choice when it comes to communication. You can develop either Yes Yes or No No speech habits.

Like it or not, your "image" and reputation depends on your choice. Just as you judge others as positive or negative by their words and actions, the same thing is happening to you.

But you can win the communications conflict by remembering to:

- Really listen when people talk.
- Stop promoting yourself above others.
- Choose Yes Yes words to express No No ideas.
- Control your voice and you'll control an argument.
- Get right to the point and state the positive facts.
- Say it with a smile.

The best time to put these ideas into practice is *right now!*

How will you react if your new radial tires won't hold air and the company refuses to give you new ones?

What will you say if your next-door neighbor shouts at you because all of your fall leaves have blown into his yard?

Every day we have great opportunities to demonstrate the value of Yes Yes listening and Yes Yes speaking. Go ahead and try it.

Start today!

5

Here Comes Good News!

We've been talking about words. But there's something that speaks much stronger and you know what it is. *Your actions*.

What you say may light a fuse, but *what you do* is the real dynamite.

In Texas I heard about a preacher in San Antonio who was ministering among the poor. He stopped in front of a run-down shack that was home for a Mexican family who had two young sons.

The younger of the two boys was a cripple.

As the minister walked up the dirt path to the door, the older brother greeted him. Then the preacher went inside to talk with the parents.

About half an hour later as he was leaving, he noticed the older brother admiring his new car.

"How do you like it, young man?"

The boy said, "It's great! Where did you get it?"

Then the reverend explained, "You know, I'm just a

minister and don't make much money. But I have a brother who lives up in Dallas who has made a lot of money in the oil business. He gave me this car."

Then the little Mexican boy looked up at the preacher and said, "I wish I could be a brother like that."

What an objective! Ninety-nine out of a hundred wish they *had* a brother like that. But here was a boy who was already rich because he wanted to *be* a brother who could give.

Let's take a look at our actions. *It's what we are that counts.*

YOUR MOST VALUABLE ASSET

Several years ago there was a young man who worked in my department at a TV station. He seemed to carry with him a spirit of perpetual optimism.

Every time Jake walked into my office I was uplifted and refreshed. He always had something good to share.

One particular morning we were having a staff meeting and as he walked in I said, "Here comes good news!"

Guess what Jake's name became around the station! "Good News." That's what they called him. And the name fit him like a glove.

What do people say when they see you coming? What is your most valuable asset?

When it comes to your reputation, it's *character*, not cash, that counts. *Your richest treasure is your attitude.* That's the way it has always been.

The Best Possible Gift

Centuries ago there was a poor artist who was entertained for a summer in a beautiful castle. When it came time to leave he realized that he had nothing to give his hosts for their hospitality.

Before he left, he shut himself in his room for several days. The door was locked.

When he finally left, the servant found the sheets of his bed missing. Were they stolen?

No!

The sheets were found by the family in the corner of the room. And when they were unrolled there was a spectacular picture of Alexander in the tent of Darius painted on them.

His most valuable asset was not his artistic ability, nor his poverty. It was his attitude. He had a desire to leave the best possible gift. And he did it without saying a word.

Yes Yes living is not something to be talked about. It is something to be *demonstrated*.

Saint Paul got right to the point when he said, "Let us not lose heart in doing good, for in due time we shall reap if we do not grow weary" (Galatians 6:9).

One of Michigan's most outstanding Avon representatives shared with me the secret of her successful business. Mayme Mayer said, "I treat my customers like I would treat my friends, because they *are* my friends."

Her business was built on *doing good things* for people, not simply selling products. She was in the *people* business, and her sales skyrocketed.

What are you doing for people?

Whether you know it or not, you are in the spotlight every day. Your actions and your attitudes are really advertisements. They are your "billboard" that is seen by more people than you imagine.

Try a Demonstration

Here's how a young man in Manhattan used his actions to help land a new job.

When a large media corporation advertised in *The New York Times* to fill an opening in its sales department, Larry Timmons replied by writing the following:

"I am presently selling furniture at the address listed below. You can judge my ability as a salesman if you will stop in to see me at any time pretending that you are interested in buying furniture.

"When you come to the store, you can identify me by my red hair. Of course, I won't have any way of knowing who you are. But what you will see is my typical sales approach and not a 'special effort' designed to impress you."

Well, you guessed it. Out of over 130 applicants for the job, Larry got it.

His actions were impressive. His attitude was affirmative. And he became a winner in life.

He asked for a positive reaction and he got it. But for some people, asking for anything seems out of the question.

For example, a salesman for a new wheel-balancing machine visited an auto repair store in Sacramento and gave the manager, Ted Stevens, a demonstration.

"Isn't it a great machine?" asked the salesman.

"Yes it is."

"It would be a great investment and a great time-

68

saver, wouldn't it?"

"Yes."

"Don't you think every garage ought to have one?"

"Yes."

"Well, why don't you buy it?"

Ted replied, "Why don't you ask me to?"

He may have believed in his wheel balancer, but he needed to ask for the order. When you believe in yourself, believe in your product and have a genuine concern for people, positive action naturally follows.

A Yes Yes attitude is your most valuable asset. And it can be yours.

WHERE DID MY ENEMIES GO?

It's rather easy to spot people living in a No No world. They are fighting a war with people. And they can always call the enemy by name.

"Mr. Hummel hates me."

"I just can't stand to be around Shirley."

"Jack is undoubtedly the most sarcastic person on earth."

"If Mrs. Anderson ever says that again, I just don't know what I'll do."

The battle lines are clearly marked and there seems to be no retreat. But instead of defeating your enemies, you can eliminate them.

Here's how Benjamin Franklin did it.

During the campaign for the Philadelphia Assembly, young Franklin was unmercifully criticized by an assemblyman. Franklin won the election but knew he had to work with his opponent.

Ben wasn't sure just why the fellow disliked him, but he knew he'd better do something about it.

Well, Franklin heard that the man had a fine library and asked if he could borrow one of his rare books. That did it! The men got to know each other because of their mutual interest in books and *he turned an enemy into a friend*.

He didn't defeat him, he *won* him.

There's Always Something to Like

It's as basic as life itself that you are attracted to some people and repulsed by others. Dealing with people is like playing with positive and negative magnets. Sometimes you are poles apart.

But no matter how much you seem to dislike a particular person, there is some quality that you can learn to appreciate.

Yes, there's always something to like. Your task is to push aside the traits and habits that upset you and *look for the good*.

Like panning for gold in a California mountain stream, it's there if you'll spend the time to search for it.

My son, Ian, attends Eugene Field School. It was named to honor the noted poet and columnist from Chicago.

One morning Field came to his office and was handed proof that his work was being plagiarized. A small-town editor was lifting his column word for word and signing his own name. But the poet didn't hit the ceiling. Instead, Field took an entire column to present a glowing tribute to that editor and lauded him as a gifted writer of unusual talent.

The plagiarist stopped immediately.

You have without doubt been faced with challenging situations. And you will continue to be tested. But why turn friends into enemies when you can turn enemies into friends?

Whatever the crisis, take a Yes Yes approach.

Sister Elizabeth Kenny, the famed Irish-Australian nurse, was asked by a friend how she managed to stay so constantly cheerful.

The friend said, "I guess you were just born calm and smiling."

"Far from it," laughed Sister Kenny. "As a girl, my temper often got out of bounds. But one day, when I became angry at a friend over some trivial matter, my mother gave me advice that I stored in my mind and have called upon for guidance ever since.

"Mother told me, 'Elizabeth, anyone who angers you, conquers you.'"

How true! You simply can't afford to surrender to anger. You'll not only lose your friends, you'll eventually turn them into enemies.

Forget Your Critics

Of course, you are going to have your critics, but when you get a great idea, start working on it.

Don't join the millions who quit before they start because they fear failure, inexperience and uncertainty. And the greatest fear is that of ridicule.

But remember this. *Your future does not depend on someone's opinion of you.* In fact, some of the world's great leaders were the target of criticism.

During the Boer War in South Africa, a young adventurer was captured, but within two weeks he escaped. His furious enemies printed "Wanted" notices.

The handbill read, "Englishman, 25 years old, about five feet eight inches tall, indifferent build, walks with a forward stoop, pale appearance, talks through his nose, and cannot pronounce the letter 's' properly."

That soldier was Winston Churchill.

It's not what people say about you that counts. Of greater importance is how you respond to what people say.

We all love praise, but some are destroyed by their own egos.

We hate criticism, but many take it far too seriously. They are also destroyed.

Perhaps Ralph Waldo Emerson found the secret when he said, "What I must do is all that concerns me, not what people think."

If your actions are dictated by the opinions of your friends, it's time for an about-face.

A friend has a motto on his desk that reads, "I respect your opinion, but I make the final decision."

You'll find that *positive decisions produce positive friends*. And you won't have to worry about enemies.

I CAN SEE IT IN YOUR FACE

Have you ever sat in a crowded room and studied the faces of people? Sure you have. And what vivid contrasts you have noticed.

One face reflects an inner calm. Another expresses

worry. A grandmother may be smiling, while a teen-ager seems to carry obvious burdens.

Your face is sending a message, too. And just as you make judgments about others, they are also "reading your face."

When Leonardo da Vinci painted "The Last Supper," he learned what a difference a facial expression can make.

To paint the face of Judas, he chose a man he despised as his "image." Then he began to paint the face of Jesus. He tried and tried to paint Christ, but just couldn't do it.

It was only after painting out the face of the man he despised and replacing it with a new image that he was able to paint the face of Jesus.

Yes, the hate he had painted wouldn't allow him to complete the picture. But he eliminated the hatred and finished the famous masterpiece.

What's Your Smile Worth?

Frowns don't produce friends! But there's something they do produce—wrinkles. An expert on aging points out that it takes 200,000 frowns to make one wrinkle. But there's no need to look old before your time. A smile can do wonders for you.

When you pause to ponder it, your smile is really worth something. It has value.

I won't soon forget the story of a little boy who was climbing a tree and came in contact with an electric wire. His face was burned and the muscle that causes him to smile was injured.

The boy had lost his smile.

The case went to the courts and the local power and light company settled the case by giving the boy $20,000.

Can you really put a price on your smile? If it's worth $20,000 when you lose it, think what it's worth when you *use* it.

Have you ever looked at someone and thought, "He has a million-dollar smile!"?

Isn't it time someone thought that about you?

Recently, while at a convention in Vancouver, British Columbia, we visited their famous Chinatown. In one store I noticed a tray marked "Worry Beads." I asked the salesgirl to tell me the benefits of the beads.

"Oh, sir," she said, "when you have tension you just move the beads on the string and the worries just go away."

Instead of buying the beads, I just laughed. And as I thought about it, I realized that my laughter was a better solution for worry than my money. Why spend it on beads?

The Doctor's Prescription

Laughter! Aristotle called it "A bodily exercise precious to health." And Dr. James Wolsh says that people who laugh "live longer than those who do not or cannot."

Have you ever considered what really happens to you when you laugh?

According to medical science it causes you to inhale and exhale in short bursts. And that increases the oxygen to your lungs and bloodstream. Your heartbeat is increased.

Laughter causes low blood pressure to rise and high blood pressure to decrease. And it accelerates your circulation. But best of all, it lifts your spirits, relieves anxiety and, like magic, helps depression disappear.

I guess *Reader's Digest* has been right all these years as they call laughter "The Best Medicine."

Adding laughter to your life should be a high priority. Surround yourself with people who are filled with joy.

Don't take life so seriously! Sure there are headlines of war, crime, hunger and inflation. And you are directly affected. But your world can be brightened by the sound of a laugh and the sight of a smile.

As the song goes, "Put on a happy face." Let the world know that something good is happening to you.

MORE GOOD NEWS!

People live in a No No world because they allow the wind, the rain, and the storms of life to determine their future. They allow people—other people—to shape their destiny.

Yes Yes living, however, is a life of self-action. There comes a time when you've got to say, "I'm the boss! It's up to me!"

I'll never forget a post-graduate course at the University of Miami called "Human Behavior."

There were seventeen of us in the course. All had received U.S. Office of Education fellowships and we represented schools and universities from several parts of the country.

The prof in that course was incredible. He opened every class with the same line: "Well, what are we going to talk about today?"

We couldn't believe it! No textbook. No course outline. No objectives written on the blackboard. No tests were scheduled.

We just talked about anything and everything.

After a couple of weeks of what we considered a waste of time, we got together after class and decided to pull off a real surprise. Bill, from Illinois, said, "Let's all read the same book over the weekend and on Monday when he asks, 'What are we going to talk about today?' let's really get into some heavy discussion."

We decided to all read B.F. Skinner's *Beyond Freedom and Dignity*.

Sure enough, he opened with his standard line on Monday and Bill said, "I've been reading Skinner, and his philosophy intrigues me." Then we all jumped in and ran the show for an hour and a half. It was one of the most lively exchanges I've ever seen in a classroom.

When it was over we decided to tell the prof what we had done.

But the biggest surprise was ours, not his! He said, "You know, it works every time. That's why this course is called Human Behavior."

For the rest of the semester we talked about what makes people tick. Our behavior was his number-one example as he proved that the learning initiated by students is far more effective than instruction determined by a teacher.

Actions *are* more effective than words.

Once we decide what we want to learn, we get excited about the educational experience. Even at the youngest ages, *learning by doing* works. And at every stage of life we want to be near the *action*.

The Best Motivation

We are motivated to "do something" by a multitude of stimuli. By love, competition, praise, and even by pride.

A physician in St. Louis discovered one Christmas that several of his patients had not paid their bills for as long as fourteen months.

During the holidays he sent each of them a letter canceling the bill with a personal handwritten note that read: "I am very sorry that you had such a poor year. I wish you and yours the very best for the coming New Year." Thirteen of the fourteen paid within one week by return mail. Their pride wouldn't have it any other way.

But there's no need for outside pressure to push you to action. Self-motivation is the best there is. It's the difference between hand-cranking a Model-T and an electronic ignition. Your "starter" needs to be on the inside.

Yes, your actions need to be determined by *you*. And it's more than what you are *thinking*, it's what you are *doing*.

Paul tells us, "And let us not lose heart in doing good, for in due time we shall reap if we do not grow weary. So then, while we have opportunity, let us do good to all men . . ." (Galatians 6:9, 10).

It Happened in Hiroshima

The war with Japan was a bitter one. It ended with an atomic explosion that was a turning point in world history.

Many years after that dreadful day, I visited a small church in Hiroshima and stood side by side with a man whose skin bore the scars of the holocaust. I talked with him after the service and he said through an interpreter, "I love the people of your country because they came to me after the war and showed me the love of God. I was in the hospital for three years. It was the help of a nurse from your country that brought me back to life."

Then he added, "Is there anything I can do for you?"

The nurse *did something*. And he wanted to do something, too.

It didn't create any headlines, but it was good news to me. I learned that no matter how chaotic the circumstance, our actions can roll back the clouds and let the sunshine in.

When the chronicle of your life is written, it will be your actions, not your words, that are recorded. Let's hope they say about you:

"He was always doing something good."

"He demonstrated an affirmative attitude."

"He was in the people business."

"His critics became his friends."

"He knew the value of laughter."

"His actions were his own."

"He always had something to give."

Those aren't the characteristics of a super-human

from an unknown planet. They can be *your* attributes. They can be *your* actions.

It may not be New Year's Day, but make a resolution to add a new dimension to your life. *Start living by giving. Dare to do!*

May it be said of you, "And in whatever he does, he prospers" (Psalm 1:3).

6

Yes Yes Living by Objectives!

On a jet bound for Europe, the pilot's voice interrupted the music on the public address system.

"Ladies and gentlemen," announced the pilot, "I have two pieces of news for you. One of them is good and the other is not so good. Let me tell you the bad news first.

"We are lost. We don't have any idea where we are. But as I told you, I have some good news, too. The good news is that we have a 200-mile-an-hour tail wind."

That's like so many people. They don't know where they are going, but they are getting there awfully fast.

What about your goals? Have you designed a road map for your life? Or are you simply wandering along an unmarked trail toward some unclear destination?

The guidance counselors of the No No world delight in telling you, "Quit while you're ahead!" "I wouldn't try that if I were you." Or, "What if you fail?"

Fail? *Never!* Not when your objectives are crystal

clear and you are doing something to achieve them.

Let's talk about your goals.

WHERE IN THE WORLD ARE YOU GOING?

Do you really know where you're headed?

I enjoy telling the story of the little sea horse who grew tired of floating around with his family. He said to his father, "Give me my inheritance. It's time for me to live my own life. I'm going to seek my fortune."

His father gave him ten gold coins and the young sea horse swam away.

Before long he met an eel who stopped him and said, "Wait just a moment. Where are you going?"

He said, "I'm going to seek my fortune."

The eel said, "If you give me three of those gold coins, I'll let you have these electric flippers that will get you there in half the time."

The sea horse gave him the coins and darted on his way.

Then, a short while later, an octopus stopped him and asked, "Where are you headed in such a hurry?"

"I'm going to seek my fortune."

"Now, if you'll give me three of those gold coins, I'll sell you this aqua-scooter that is the fastest thing in the ocean."

The sea horse smiled, gave him the coins and was on his way—even faster.

He hadn't gone far, however, when he was stopped by a shark who asked, "Where in the world are you going?"

"I'm going to seek my fortune."

"Well," said the shark, "if you'll give me those four gold coins, I'll show you a shortcut that will get you there in a hurry."

The sea horse handed him the last of his coins and the shark gave the directions.

The sea horse did as he was told. He put the aquascooter in high gear, activated his electric flippers and followed the directions—right into the open jaws of that shark.

The poor little sea horse was never to be heard from again.

Now the moral of the story is this: *If you don't know where you're going, you'll never recognize your destination when you arrive.*

Field Sent a Message

I've met people who are just like that little creature of the sea. They are in a big hurry, but have absolutely no idea where they're headed.

Man's greatest progress has been marked by people who have a specific goal to do a specific job. And they can tell you exactly what that objective is.

Cyrus Field became possessed with the idea that a cable could be laid on the bottom of the Atlantic Ocean that would allow telegraphic communication between Europe and the United States. "I know we can do it," said Field.

He had the special cable manufactured and began to lay it. But the attempt to span the two continents failed time after time. Headlines read, "Field Fails Again."

His friends were disheartened. The public was

skeptical and his investors refused to risk any more money.

But the ridicule only served to strengthen his conviction. Give up? Not Field! He organized a new company, designed a new cable and it worked! A message could be transmitted by wire beneath an entire ocean.

The first message sent on the cable was this: "Thank God, the cable is laid and is in perfect order." There were shouts of joy on the other end.

Field knew he would ultimately win. His goal had gripped him with conviction. To him it was an *attainable goal*. It was also a *measurable goal*.

Promise vs. Performance

When the Federal Communications Commission reviews a radio or TV station for license renewal they employ a technique known as "promise vs. performance."

Here's how it works. When a station is granted a license it makes *promises* concerning its programming, public service, community involvement, etc. Then, during the review for renewal, the commission measures the promises in light of the actual *performance*.

Goals are great, but your life is not measured by your objectives, but by what you are doing to achieve them.

If you are a waitress and your objective is to get tips, *you'll go broke*. But if your goal is to give great service, you will be measured by your performance and you'll

84

never have to worry about tips.

Whether your goals are short term or long term, the most important fact is that you have them.

It is difficult to comprehend, but there are thousands of adults in the United States who have never had a goal to learn to read or write. How is it possible?

I listened to a man who confessed that he was a functional illiterate as a teenager. At seventeen, he lied about his age and joined the Navy.

There, for the first time in his life, he was confronted with a problem he really wanted to solve. The lighting system where he was working needed to be fixed. He got a manual about lighting and *learned to read* simply because *he wanted to.*

Within fourteen years he was Dr. Capp, a Ph.D. He told us, "Nothing really happens until you *want* it to happen. And once you set a goal, there's no stopping."

Have you determined what you really *want* to happen? Is your objective clear? *Are you doing something to achieve it?*

THE GREATEST GOAL IN THE WORLD

There are thousands of objectives you can choose in life, but one goal should stand above all others.

The greatest goal is to have an *honest* goal. Yes, "To thine own self be true." Of what value is an objective that is not based on *truth,* on *right,* on *virtue?*

There's a lesson we can learn from the senior in a Philadelphia high school who answered an ad for a job as a clerk in a downtown candy store.

The owner thought he'd found the perfect employee

and began to share his sales techniques.

"Don't tell the customer too much. And by the way, don't worry if you fudge on the weights. Let me show you a little trick. After all, we've got to make a profit, you know."

Finally, the owner asked, "Young man, how much do you expect in the way of pay?"

Without hesitating, the student said, "$100,000." Then he added, "Sir, you couldn't pay me enough to be a liar for you. I wouldn't do that for *any* amount."

Take a look at your goal. Is it an *honest* goal? Is it based on truth?

"We're Number Two"

One of the most successful media campaigns ever conducted was designed by the New York advertising agency of Doyle Dane Bernbach. They were given the goal of taking a second-rate auto leasing firm and improving its image.

They created the slogan, "We're Number Two," that made Avis a household word.

The agency analyzed Avis' situation and concluded that the only way to promote it was to come on honestly and declare that their client was only the second largest car rental agency, but that *it tried harder*.

Warren Avis, the founder of the company, says, *"It was no magic formula—just the truth."*

It worked for Avis, and it will work for you, too.

I laughed, however, when I heard about the conference that was called to protest "deceptive packaging" of consumer goods.

A survey of the women attending the meeting revealed that 15 percent tinted their hair, 38 percent wore wigs, 80 percent wore eye shadow, and 93 percent painted their nails.

The conference concluded with a resolution condemning "any form of false packaging." It passed by 100 percent!

At least their heart was in the right place!

Get a goal that is based on honesty and integrity. It is essential in your personal life and invaluable in the business world.

Cliff Jones, chairman of the board for Jones and Babson, the management company of Babson Mutual Funds, recently spoke to the Kansas City Rotary Club.

He placed executives into two groups. Type "A" he described as "financially insecure, fearful, and the classic profile of a loser."

His type "B" was just the opposite. "He is the 'can do' person with real goals."

Says Jones, "With a management team composed of only type 'A' executives, fear is very apt to permeate the whole company. Such fear usually leads to scheming and manipulation, up and down the organizational ladder."

And here was his conclusion. "I suggest the answer in a nutshell is that the best fuel for any organization is a positive moral commitment starting with the top brass."

Furs, Fortune, and Freedom

To do things right, you've got to *be* right. It starts on

the *inside*. Goals you feel with your heart and know to be honest are the only objectives worth your time.

Consider the goals of those early settlers of America.

The French came to the heartland of the continent. They were looking for furs.

The Spanish came to the tropics of Florida. They were looking for fortune.

But the Pilgrims landed on the rocky coast of the Northeast. They were looking for freedom.

What was the difference? How could the passengers of the Mayflower succeed when others had failed? *Their objective was spiritual.* Their goal was based on God's direction for their lives. They sought freedom to worship and they prevailed in a No No world.

The greatest objectives are reached by the heart, not by the head. It's time to take a new look at your goals.

HERE'S HOW IT WORKS

I've seen dozens of prescriptions for happiness. There have been countless books written on the topic. But the only "secret" that ever caught my attention was written by John Burrows who said, *"Happiness is something to do."*

Think about it! Your greatest contentment comes from working toward your goal. That's the *real* achievement.

I've seen some of the magnificent sculptures of Michelangelo and thought, "I'll bet he was a proud man when he finished that statue." I could imagine him standing back and admiring it.

But that's not the way it was. Michelangelo said, "It

is only well with me when I have a chisel in my hand."

Oh, it's essential to have a goal, but getting there is much more than half the fun. The man who inspired Browning, Dickens and Tennyson was Thomas Carlyle. His philosophy still holds true: "Get your happiness out of your work or you will never know what real happiness is."

Monday morning blues? Forget about them. You are the richest person alive just to be able to tackle that task.

You say, "But I wish I could just stay in bed and have people wait on me all day!" Well, sir, the hospitals are filled with people just like that who would gladly trade places with you.

The Cure Called "Work"

Recently I was browsing through some old books and came across a poem by an unknown author. The message gets right to the point:

If you are rich, work.
If you are burdened with seemingly unfair
    responsibilities, work.
If you are happy, continue to work;
Idleness gives room for doubts and fears.
If sorrow overwhelms you and loved ones
    seem not true, work.
If disappointments come, work.
If faith falters and reason fails, just work.
When dreams are shattered and hope
    seems dead,

Work, work as if your life were in peril;
It really is.
No matter what ails you, work.
Work faithfully and work with faith.
Work is the greatest material
   remedy available.
Work will cure both mental and
   physical afflictions.
Work!

What does the Word say? "Whatever your hand finds to do, verily, do it with all your might" (Ecclesiastes 9:10).

Reaching your goal takes more than a dream. The earth won't turn until your hand is on the plow. And then you've got to push with all the power you can provide.

Somewhere along the line, however, we've lost our backbone.

Last summer, a farmer near Chicago placed a classified ad in the "Help Wanted" column of the *Tribune*. It read, "Needed, Workers to pick 90 acres of strawberries. Minimum wage." He gave his phone number.

I was shocked to learn that he had to plow under 90 acres of rotten strawberries. *Not one person responded!*

In a city with high unemployment and thousands on welfare, nobody wanted to work. What a tragedy!

Our nation was built on a strong work ethic, but there are millions who will offer any excuse to avoid tackling a task.

Do It Anyway

When LeBaron Briggs was the academic dean at Harvard, a graduate student came to his office to explain why he failed to complete his master's thesis on time. The student told him, "I haven't been feeling well."

Dean Briggs replied, "Young man, I think it's time you realize that most of the work done in this world is done by people who aren't feeling well."

Why not adopt the "do it anyway" philosophy. It's a sure way to reach your goal. No matter what the objective, it's going to take perspiration to get there.

Right now, take the time to write one of your personal goals on a piece of paper. Then under that objective make a list of the things you must do to accomplish it.

There it is in black and white! Those "steps" on your ladder must be climbed. And whether the work is done next week or next year, it *still must be done.* So why not begin to do the required work *today?*

The same goal can take twenty days or twenty years. It depends on when you do the work.

The famous British Poet Laureate, John Masefield, was asked, "What inspires you to do your work?" His reply was a little poem by an unknown author:

Sitting still and wishing
Makes no person great.
The good Lord sends the fishing
But you must dig the bait!

91

Masefield was often discouraged, but he always remembered those words.

Name your goal and it will be clear that some digging is involved. Begin to do it! A little today, a little tomorrow. Great monuments are not built in a day. They are built one stone at a time.

Work! That's the irreplaceable ingredient.

GOAL TO GO!

Today, you need to do something specific to help you reach your number-one goal.

What is that objective! Can you describe it? Do you see it clearly?

Most people waste all of the 86,400 seconds they are granted each day. We usually don't think in terms of seconds or even minutes. Instead we fill hours of time with activities seldom related to that goal tucked away in our minds.

It reminds me of the three boys who were playing in the snow. A man walked up and said, "Would you like to try a new kind of race? I'll give the winner a prize."

The boys quickly agreed and the man told them that his race would be one that required skill. "I will go to the other side of the field," he explained, "and when I give you the signal, you will start to run. The one whose footsteps are the straightest in the snow will be declared the winner."

The race began, and the first boy kept looking at his feet to see if his steps were straight.

The second fellow kept looking at his friends to see what they were doing.

But the third boy won the race because his steps were straight in the snow. He didn't look down. He didn't look around. *He kept his eyes firmly on the objective.*

There is a powerful lesson you can learn from the boys. Why not put it into practice?

Today, make your minutes count. Keep moving toward your goal.

Say Yes and Stick To It

Once you know your goal, don't let anyone stop you from attaining it.

Henry Ward Beecher, the great orator, recalled the day in school when he was demonstrating a problem in geometry. The teacher stopped him with a "No, No!" in a tone of total conviction.

Beecher sat down in total confusion because he thought he was doing it right.

The next boy went to the board and was stopped with the same loud "No!" But he went right ahead, completed the geometry problem, and sat down.

Beecher raised his hand and told his teacher, "I did exactly what he did, but you said No."

The teacher replied, "Why didn't you say Yes and stick to it? It's not good enough to know your lesson. You must *know* you know it."

You haven't really learned anything until you are sure of it. If the whole world says "No, No!" you can say "Yes, Yes!" and persist in your belief.

"Everybody's out to stop me! Nobody wants me to reach my goal!" If that's what you're thinking, *you're exactly right.*

The Pittsburgh Steelers can tell you the same thing. Every time they try to reach that end zone there are eleven tough guys and a few striped shirts out to make sure they earn every inch of it.

But whether it's football, hockey, Ping Pong, or life itself, there is no victory without a struggle.

It's how you react to the battle that builds character. Some turn in their battle gear at spring training. But the champions fight all odds to stand in the winners' circle.

Every day, your actions determine whether or not you'll reach that goal.

Prison or Palace?

You are actually building the house you live in. It's like the story of a man who became trapped while trying to reach his goal. He built an iron cage around himself in which he was doomed to spend the rest of his life.

As a young boy, he wasted his time and a bar of "idleness" was in front of him which prevented any great accomplishment.

The next bar on the cage was "untidiness," which kept refined and successful people away from him.

He erected a bar of "disagreeableness" between himself and the world by his overbearing, conceited and discourteous manner.

A bar of "distrust" was built by his dishonesty. It separated him from upright and honest people.

His gluttony and intemperance built a bar that made him incapable of physical activity.

The bars he had erected finally made him a prisoner.

Every act of life seems to drive a nail in your character. What are you building? Is it a prison? Or is it a palace?

Set your goals high and begin to live a life that will allow you to reach them.

If you don't have an objective, you'll reach that, too. "You do not have because you do not ask" (James 4:2).

But let the Lord inspire you with his message of faith: "Truly I say unto you, whoever says to this mountain, 'Be taken up and cast into the sea,' and does not doubt in his heart, but believes that what he says is going to happen, it shall be granted him.

"Therefore I say to you, all things for which you pray and ask, believe that you have received them, and they shall be granted you" (Mark 11:23, 24).

Again, let me ask, "What is your goal?"

Is your objective clear?

Can you measure your progress?

Is it an honest goal?

Are you working at it?

Is it based on spiritual principles?

Do you really believe it will happen?

Aim as high as you can. Work as hard as you can. And the goal that others call "impossible" will be yours for the asking.

You can do it!

7

Say Thanks
for Your Problems!

In Omaha, a young man got off the hospital elevator on the wrong floor. He suddenly heard dozens of babies crying and asked the nurse, "What's going on? What's all the crying about?"

"You'd cry too," she said, "if you had just arrived and found you owed the government thousands of dollars on the national debt and had wet pants."

Problems are nothing new. You were born with them and they will be with you for life. People problems. Money problems. Health problems. They come in all shapes, sizes, and degrees of difficulty.

But there is no need to panic over pain and hardship. Your trials are there for a definite purpose.

Your problems cause you to "grow up." *They are opportunities in disguise. They keep you alert and alive.*

Instead of throwing in the towel, it's time to look up and say "Thanks!"

Yes, you have a problem and *that can be one of the most exciting experiences of your life.*

WHAT'S THE BIG PROBLEM?

Have you ever met a person who delights in telling you all the details of why they can't be a success? Or someone who can tell you their complete medical history—and all of it is bad?

Sure you have.

To them, problems are not opportunities, they are excuses. And their joy is not to triumph over trials, but rather to revel in their misery.

Edward Everett Hale had this advice for folks who expect the worst. He said, "We should never attempt to bear more than one kind of trouble at once. Some people bear all three kinds—all they *have had*, all they *now have*, and all they *expect to have*."

That's triple trouble!

Hale, who wrote *The Man Without a Country*, had a tranquilizer for trouble. Instead of drowning in his own problems, he rose to the top by helping someone else. He was a leader in the "Lend a Hand" movement, whose motto was, "Look up and not down, forward and not back, look out and not in, lend a hand."

You're going to have problems, but there's no need to multiply them. One at a time is plenty. But you can decrease your difficulties by taking the time to help someone else. Instead of dwelling on your own dilemma, why not reach out and give someone your hand?

Better Than Being Ignored

Life's most perplexing problems usually come in the form of *people*.

The fellow who brags, "Everybody likes me; I don't have an enemy on earth," had better be careful. When that's the case, you can bet he's not accomplishing much.

If your biggest problem is that someone doesn't exactly like you, give yourself a round of applause. Anyone who is a real success is bound to be the object of jealousy.

Why not make the best of it? After all, your enemies keep you on your toes. Their envy can cause you to work harder than you ever imagined.

Enemies are great as long as you fight *yourself* and don't battle *them*. Just let their attitude serve to sharpen your skills and to increase your abilities.

As someone remarked, "Cherish your enemies. At least they don't try to hit you for a loan."

Instead of fuming at those who would put you down, consider it a unique form of flattery. After all, if they weren't concerned with your opinion, they would just ignore you.

Put your problems with people in a new perspective. *They are great opportunities for you to get to know someone much better*. Perhaps that someone is *yourself*.

The "Decision Dodgers"

Whatever the problem, there comes a moment of decision when you've got to make that difficult choice. For many, that's the roughest problem of all.

In the business world, decisions have to be made by the dozens every day. But some take the ostrich approach and stick their heads in the sand. Have you ever met a "decision dodger"?

Executive's Digest lists ten ways to avoid making a decision.

1. Delegate the problem to a committee.
2. Give an answer in double talk.
3. Delegate the problem to a subordinate.
4. Have a "study" made to get all the facts.
5. Indicate that all problems must be dealt with in numerical order.
6. Call in an expert to make sure "we're on solid ground."
7. Immediately get sick.
8. Arrange to be called out of town.
9. Deny the problem exists.
10. Put on your coat and go home.

Perhaps an eleventh rule should be added: "Start looking for another job." *If you can't make firm choices, don't expect to be the choice of the firm.*

Those who inhabit the No No world are easy to identify. They're holding a magnifying glass, carrying a baseball bat, and wearing track shoes.

The glass enlarges their problem. The bat is used on enemies, and the shoes speed them away from decisions.

But that's not you! Problems are yours for a purpose. You accept them because they give you a chance to defeat discouragement, to make new friends, and to make decisions. *They give you a chance to win.*

It's a great opportunity!

POSITIVELY HANDICAPPED!

While it is true that everybody has problems, some have severe physical handicaps that would cause most people to give up.

One out of every seven people in our world has a disability. There are over 30 million handicapped Americans and over 10 million have disabilities that should keep them from leading a normal life.

But don't be fooled by the statistics. For some it should be spelled "handy-capped." Their problem became a springboard to success.

Arturo Toscanini is a great example of a man who turned a problem into a blessing. He owed his success to the fact that he was extremely nearsighted.

At the age of nineteen he was playing cello in an orchestra. But since he couldn't see the music on the stand, he listened to it and memorized it.

One evening, just before a major performance, the director suddenly became ill and young Toscanini was the only person in the orchestra who knew the score.

He conducted it "by heart" and the audience loved it.

Just think! If he hadn't been nearsighted, he may have spent his life playing cello. But instead, he was hailed as one of the greatest orchestral conductors the world has ever known.

He knew the score!

The Noise Didn't Bother Him

For several years I taught a college-level course in public speaking and I can vividly recall several students who had some form of a handicap. One with a cleft pallet. An amputee. A blind student.

But what I remember most is that the handicapped did not depend on sympathy for a good grade. They made extraordinary progress because they worked harder than the "normal" student.

I've seen it over and over again as the gifted, talented student made only marginal progress, but for the handicapped, the gains were great.

When Bruce Stubbs stepped on the basketball court for the Evangel "Crusaders," he became one of the most unique players on the hardwood.

For most players, basketball is a game of fans screaming, bands blaring, coaches shouting, and referees blowing their whistles. But not for Stubbs.

Bruce is deaf.

When he was five years old, he fell while playing in a tree. The accident left him totally deaf in one ear and with just 10 percent hearing in the other. The only sound he hears is a combination of buzzing and vibrations.

But Bruce developed some skills that made people forget about his handicap. He can "read lips" as well as some people can hear. That's how he coped in the classroom.

In addition to being deaf, he's only 5' 11", and that's a little short for today's basketball players. But in high school at Winter Haven, Florida, he worked on his jumping ability. During his freshman year at Evangel the fans were shocked to see him out-jump and out-rebound players a foot taller. In fact, he set the school's season single-game record by grabbing eighteen rebounds despite an opposing 6'11" player fighting him under the basket.

Bruce just smiles when someone talks about his hearing problem. As he communicated to his coach, "At least the crowd noise doesn't bother me."

To Bruce it's not a handicap. It's a challenge.

Ralph Waldo Emerson was right when he wrote, "For everything you have missed, you have gained something else."

Nothing's Going to Stop You

Even people suffering from a serious illness can rise above it.

Phil Scaffidi became one of the outstanding players on the Niagara University basketball team. And that was *after* he lost 60 percent of his liver and parts of other organs undergoing major cancer surgery.

He was forced to wear heavy braces on both knees to fight arthritis brought on by chemotherapy. But that didn't hinder his desire to excel.

Niagara's coach Dan Raskin says, "He doesn't let his problem affect what he's doing and he doesn't use it as a crutch in life." Then he added, "If my son could grow up to be Phil Scaffidi, I'd be a very happy man."

Bruce and Phil have said "Yes" when others have said "No." They refused to allow their physical problems to be negative factors in their lives.

Regardless of the difficulties that come your way, you've got to say, "OK. This is *me*, and *I'm going to give it my best*."

As psychologist William James put it, "Acceptance

of what has happened is the first step to overcoming the consequences of any misfortune."

Why blame yourself? Why blame your problem? Why blame God?

Instead, trade your blaming for a blessing. Go ahead and accept your present state and watch what can happen.

Epictetus, the first-century stoic Greek philosopher, believed that <u>only foolish</u> people are upset by events they cannot control.

Listen to what he says: "Sickness is a hindrance to the body, but not the will, unless the will consent. Lameness is a hindrance to the leg, but not the will. Say this to yourself at each event that happens, for you shall find that though it hinders something else, it will not hinder *you*."

Which is the greatest handicap, a broken bone or a broken spirit? *A loss of health is nothing when compared with a loss of heart*.

Yes, you can bounce back. And you have help. "I can do all things through Him who strengthens me" (Philippians 4:13).

SOLVING THE PUZZLE

While some are handicapped physically, even more are disabled *emotionally*. On the surface, they might look quite calm, but inside a war is raging. Let's hope that you are not a prisoner of that emotional war.

What is your response to a personal crisis? How do you react to problems that seem bigger than life itself?

"Falling apart" just won't do. It's time to put the

pieces of the puzzle back together. *Relax!* The solution to your problem may be easier than you think.

Charles Kettering, the great inventor, had a rather unique method of solving problems. He would take the *big* problem and break it down into the smallest possible "sub-problems."

On each of the mini-problems, he did research to see which of these *had already been solved.* To his amazement, he found that what at first looked like a gigantic problem, was not so bad after all. Kettering found that *98 percent of most problems had already been solved by others.* All he had to do was to tackle what was left.

The Ohio inventor used his reasoning method to develop ethyl gasoline, quick-drying lacquer, and the two-cycle diesel engine.

Kettering not only invented the automobile self-starter—he *was* one. Bad eyesight slowed his education, but he didn't let it stop him.

Why not follow the inventor's method? *Take the problem apart and work on it piece by piece*. It's amazing how things will start coming together.

The Ant and the Straw

Stay calm! The solution to your dilemma might be within your grasp. In fact, the problem itself may be your solution.

A biologist in Madison, Wisconsin, told how he watched a tiny ant pick up a piece of straw 100 times his size. He watched with fascination. What a burden he was carrying!

Where was he going with it? "I watched as the ant

came to a crack in the ground. It was far too wide for him to get across. So the ant carefully laid the piece of straw across the gap and walked on it to the other side."

Then the biologist added, "What appeared to be a burden for the ant was actually his escape."

Yes, *your problem may be your solution*.

Don't despair when you're faced with a question that seems to have no answer. There *is* a way out. And you should start by looking at the problem itself.

When Alton Bell was a freshman at Southern Illinois University, he enrolled in a math course that proved to be tougher than he could imagine.

Two days before a major exam on "plane trigonometry," he faced another pressure point. On the same day of the math exam he had a 2,000-word original essay due for English Composition 101.

Alton had a flash of inspiration! He immediately began to write the English paper on the topic "Plane Trigonometry Made Plain." In the simplest language possible he explained how astronomers, navigators, and surveyors use ratios to compute the relations between the sides of a right triangle. Even Alton could understand it! He got an "A" on the theme and a "B" on the test.

His problem with math became his answer for writing. But even better, it was his solution for math, too.

For most of life's puzzles, there is no reason to panic. As French statesman Jean Monnet observed, "There are no misfortunes, only ill health and death."

Watch Your Troubles Disappear

The day-to-day problems you face aren't worth getting upset about. In fact, there's a phrase you should add to your vocabulary: "No problem."

Sink stopped up? "No problem."

Flat tire? "No problem."

Paint on the carpet? "No problem."

Why waste your mental and emotional energies on minor mishaps that will be forgotten tomorrow?

In Formosa, I heard about a fellow who has an unusual way of getting rid of problems.

While walking home from work each evening he stops at a certain tree, takes out a piece of paper and writes down all of his troubles. Then he ties the paper to one of the branches and says, "I'm finished with those for today."

He calls it his "Trouble Tree."

The next day he stops at the tree again. But he says, "Four out of five nights my troubles have blown away by morning. And when I read my old list, the problems don't seem too great at all."

It's true. *Most of your problems will disappear on their own* if you'll let them. Your best tranquilizer is *time*. Sit back and watch the puzzle come together.

Begin to feel that Yes Yes assurance that everything is going to work out fine.

YES, THERE'S A RAINBOW

When I was just a boy I heard my father tell the story of Captain Eddie Rickenbacker. His ordeal during World War II was unforgettable.

Rickenbacker, the leading air ace of World War I who became president of Eastern Airlines, was asked in 1942 to make an inspection trip of U.S. forces in the Pacific battle zones.

He and seven others were flying about 600 miles north of Samoa when their plane was shot down.

Eight men in three tiny rafts. For eight days they survived on four little oranges.

The sun was burning them. Delirium was setting in. But the captain believed in prayer. And one of his men had a small Bible they used as they held morning and evening prayer meetings.

On the eighth day they read from the Lord's Sermon on the Mount: "Therefore take no thought, saying, What shall we eat? or, What shall we drink . . . ?" And they read, "Take therefore no thought for the morrow: for the morrow shall take thought for the things of itself . . ." (Matthew 6:31, 34 KJV).

What happened next was incredible! A seagull appeared out of the blue sky and landed on Rickenbacker's head. Very gently he reached up and grabbed it.

They ate it raw—even the bones. It was enough food for two days. And they took the gull's innards for bait, made a hook out of a piece of wire and caught a small mackerel and a sea bass.

Suddenly a single cloud appeared and poured fresh water into their rafts.

After twenty-four days they were rescued and the headlines read, "WE PRAYED!"

Does God answer prayer? To Captain Rickenbacker there was no question. It holds the answer for your problem, too. "And everything you ask in prayer, believing, you shall receive" (Matthew 21:22).

A Motto Fit for a King

There is an answer to your problems, your pressures, your trials and tears. Your highest mountain really can be cast into the sea.

Your problems *will* pass.

Your pressures *will* ease.

Your trials *will* end.

Your tears *will* dry.

When it seems there is no end in sight, remember the story of an Eastern king who lived centuries ago. His life was filled with problems of all kinds.

One morning he called his wise men together and asked, "Can you create a motto or phrase that will help me through my times of distress?"

He gave them rules for creation of the motto: "It must be brief enough to inscribe on my golden ring. It must apply to every situation. It must work in good times and in bad times. It must be valid for every circumstance."

The wise men went away for more than a month. And when they returned they presented the magic phrase to the king.

Here it is! "This, too, shall pass away!"

Now that's a phrase to remember. Whatever the crisis, the fog will lift, the clouds will part, and you'll see a rainbow.

Longfellow put it this way, "The lowest ebb is the turn of the tide."

You Know Who the Winner Is

Since you *know* that things are going to get better. Since you *know* the tide will turn. Since you *know* God answers prayer. Why not look at your problem from "tomorrow's vantage point." View the battle from the victor's side.

You can smile through your darkest hour knowing who is going to win the conflict.

Problems? They are real and you know it. But you can say "Thanks" because of the rich new dimension they add to your life.

The next time you are faced with an "insurmountable" hurdle, remember this:

- Problems are yours for a purpose.
- Difficulties give you a chance to develop.
- A handicap can be your greatest blessing.
- Nothing can stop your will to win.
- Solve the puzzle one piece at a time.
- The problem itself may be the solution.
- Pray! Give God a chance to answer.
- Relax! This, too, shall pass away.

When the situation seems hopeless and your options seem few, look up and hear Christ say, "My peace I give to you . . . Let not your heart be troubled, nor let it be fearful" (John 14:27).

Yes, there is a rainbow.

8

The World's Greatest Commandment

Every night, Terry knelt at the side of his bed, closed his eyes and prayed, "God bless mom. God bless dad. God bless grandma." He said it the same way every time.

But one night he added, "And please take care of yourself, God. 'Cause if anything happened to you, we're all sunk!"

How true!

If I were asked to give only one requisite for successful living, it would be this: *Faith in God.* "For in Him we live and move and exist . . ." (Acts 17:28).

Let's face the facts! The evidence is clear that those who believe in a living God have added a power to their lives that defies explanation. And millions of people stand tall as they declare, "Yes, I am a Christian."

That's right. Top leaders everywhere declare without hesitation, "I have accepted God's Son, Jesus, as my personal Savior." To be "born again" is more than adopting a phrase. *It is real!* I know. It happened to me.

There are those who would argue the facts, but as it's been said, "The man with an experience is never at the mercy of the man with an argument."

If you've made a spiritual commitment, there is no point in hiding it. It's part of *you*, and the world needs to know it.

You say, "It's impossible! No one can live up to God's laws. No one can even keep the Ten Commandments."

Hang on! That's what we're going to talk about. It gets right to the heart of Yes Yes living.

THE YES YES COMMANDMENT

The Bible is filled with hundreds of laws. Rules covering government, citizenship, taxation, crime, marriage, parents, inheritance, real estate, contracts, social security, and the list seems endless. But at Mount Sinai, God gave Moses His divine laws. They were etched in stone and we know them as the Ten Commandments. Here they are:

1. Thou shalt have no other gods before me.
2. Thou shalt not make unto thee any graven image.
3. Thou shalt not take the name of the Lord thy God in vain.
4. Remember the sabbath day to keep it holy.
5. Honor thy father and thy mother.
6. Thou shalt not kill.
7. Thou shalt not commit adultery.
8. Thou shalt not steal.
9. Thou shalt not bear false witness.
10. Thou shalt not covet. (Exodus 20:3-17 KJV)

Is it any wonder that people find these laws difficult to keep? Nobody likes restrictions. We don't like being told what we cannot do.

Three No No words are repeated over and over again. "Thou shalt *not.*" "Thou shalt *not.*" "Thou shalt *not.*"

But wait! The Law of Moses isn't the end of the story. Something happened to change darkness into light.

Much More Than a Word

Christ came to lift the restrictions of the law. He not only completed it, He *replaced* it. "A new commandment I give to you, that you love one another, even as I have loved you . . ." (John 13:34).

The negatives of the commandments were replaced with one Yes Yes word. That word is *love!*

Scripture clearly states that "love . . . is the fulfillment of the law" (Romans 13:10).

But it's much more than a word. It is the most powerful force you'll ever know. And when you apply it, feel it, use it, and *know* it, your negatives will disappear, too. That's why it is called "a more excellent way."

When Christ was asked by a lawyer to name "the greatest commandment," He didn't say, "Thou shalt not." Instead, He quoted Deuteronomy 6:8 and said, "You shall love the Lord your God with all your heart, and with all your soul, and with all your mind. This is the greatest and foremost commandment" (Matthew 22:37, 38).

Then he added, "And a second is like it, 'You shall love your neighbor as yourself'" (v. 39).

Think about what he said. *Love God and love your neighbor.* Isn't that what it's all about?

In fact, the *only* way to keep the Ten Commandments is to keep the "greatest" commandment. Love makes it easy.

The Ten "I Will" Commandments

If you love the Lord with your heart, soul, and mind, "thou shalt not" becomes "I will." They will suddenly be *your* commandments.

1. I will serve only one God.
2. I will worship Him in spirit and in truth.
3. I will praise His name.
4. I will keep God's day sacred.
5. I will respect my parents.
6. I will respect and preserve life.
7. I will be faithful in marriage.
8. I will work for what I need.
9. I will tell the truth.
10. I will be content with what I have.

When the Love Commandment is kept, the Ten Commandments become new. Suddenly they are transformed into positive commitments you *want* to keep because you are motivated by love.

Yes, faith in God is a requirement for successful living, but what brings it to life is the fact that God *is* love.

I remember a sign on a church marquee in Milwaukee: "Love is more than a characteristic of God. It is His character."

Is it also your character?

You'll never know the Yes Yes life until God's love becomes *your* love. And once you accept it, your life is transformed.

Compassion will replace conflict.

Generosity will replace greed.

Humility will replace haughtiness.

Courtesy will replace contempt.

Those you meet will feel the difference when love is the motivation for your actions.

What did Paul tell the Corinthians? "And if I give all my possessions to feed the poor . . . but do not have love, it profits me nothing." And he added, "But now abide faith, hope, love, these three; but the greatest of these is love" (1 Corinthians 13:3, 13).

It's the easiest commandment you've ever tried to keep. *Love!*

WHAT A DIFFERENCE A WORD MAKES

Is it possible that one small word can have such an impact on your life? Can it really turn your life around? Is "love" that powerful?

Let me tell you what happened at a large steel factory just outside Pittsburgh, Pennsylvania.

A rough iron worker named Ralph had an uncontrollable temper and could hardly speak ten words without swearing or using blasphemy.

But something happened to Ralph. He had a conversion experience that literally turned his life around. God's love had conquered him and he began to live by the "greatest" commandment.

When the news hit the factory, the men on his shift watched him closely. They were waiting for his temper to flare and for him to fill the air with cursing.

It didn't happen, so the men prepared a trap for Ralph. While he was taking his afternoon coffee break, they heated a long bar of iron and tempered it to look as though it were cold. Then they laid it on the floor near his working spot and waited for him to pick it up.

When Ralph returned, he bent over and grabbed the hot iron with both hands.

Immediately, his hands blistered and the men expected him to explode with rage. But Ralph turned around and quietly said, "Men, I didn't think you would do that."

One by one, the men apologized. Some had tears in their eyes as they realized that this wasn't the "old Ralph," this was a "new Ralph."

He had been transformed by God's love. And now *His* love was being demonstrated.

The Eagle and the Baby

Yes, love can tame a temper, but its power goes far beyond that.

When I was a boy, I remember hearing a story that happened long ago in Scotland.

One day a great eagle swooped down from the sky and carried away a tiny baby boy who was sleeping on the front porch of his mother's cottage. Nearly everyone in the village ran after it, but the eagle soon placed the baby high up on a cliff, near its nest.

It quickly became evident that the baby might never

be recovered. A strong sailor tried to climb the cliff, but his limbs began to tremble and he had to give up the attempt. Then a shepherd, accustomed to climbing, tried. But after a short distance he lost his footing and fell to the bottom of the cliff.

At last a poor peasant woman tried. She put her feet on one shelf of the rock, then on another, then on a third. Those who were watching felt their hearts pounding with fear.

Slowly she climbed higher and higher until she reached the eagle's nest at the top of the cliff. She took the baby in her arms, then step by step, she began the dangerous descent. She moved slowly and carefully. Finally, she stood at the bottom of the cliff with the little boy safe in her arms.

Why did the peasant woman succeed when the strong sailor and the experienced shepherd had failed? It was because of the strong link of love which bound her to the child.

She was the baby's mother.

That's what love can do.

Whether it's between parent and child, husband and wife, teacher and student, employer and employee, or between neighbors, nothing can substitute for genuine love.

It's Not a One-Way Street

As you put it into practice, love takes many forms.

It means *caring* when someone is in pain. *Sharing* in their need. *Confiding* in their trust. *Rejoicing* in their success. Love means *feeling* what they feel.

You may have the "textbook" formula for success: a great desire, a strong will, the sharpest wardrobe, a big smile and even a fat bank account, but if you don't have love it's worthless. Your success will be hollow. Your victory will be in vain.

Sure you've got to look out for your own interests. But when it comes to love, it's not a one-way street. The road leads *out*, and it leads *up*.

The great expositor Sam Shoemaker put it this way: "In the triangle of love between ourselves, God, and other people, is found the secret of existence, and the best foretaste of what heaven will probably be like."

Let love be at the center of your life. What a difference it will make!

LEARNING TO LOVE

It's amazing how things look new when viewed through the eyes of love. People you "can't stand" suddenly have an attraction. A job you loathe will take on meaning and purpose.

Let me tell you about a fellow in Oregon who took great pride in his lawn. But one summer he had a heavy crop of dandelions. They were growing faster than he could kill them. He tried everything imaginable to get rid of them.

Finally he wrote the agriculture department, telling them all the things he had tried. He concluded his letter by asking, "What in the world should I do now?"

Well, the next week he had his reply. "We suggest you learn to love them."

There's so much in life that can upset you. The No No

world is filled with hatred, disgust, anxiety and despair. There's a waiting list to join the "Moan and Groan Society."

But why not end your sulking and let your spirits soar. You can, by learning to love those things you call "problems."

Too Much of a Good Thing

Come alive! Let love show the way and watch your life begin to grow.

But wait! When it comes to love, the directions say, "easy does it." You can give too much of a good thing.

I remember the first time I planted tomatoes in the backyard. I turned the soil, put up the stakes, and carefully placed those tender plants in the soil.

Oh, how I wanted them to grow. So I poured a full cup of fertilizer on every plant and gave them plenty of water.

I'll never forget what happened. For the next five days I watched with pride as those little plants literally sprang up from the ground. They were growing like nothing I'd ever seen. Then it happened! Suddenly, the plants fell over limp. Every one of them. They all died!

I asked my neighbor, "What happened?" And when he found out how much fertilizer I used, he laughed and said, "You know, you can overdo a good thing."

But just like nature, love can't be rushed. You've got to aim for steady growth. No matter what happens, just keep right on loving. Through good times or bad. Through triumph or torment. Don't slow your steady stream of love. And just watch what happens.

It's like the sign I saw hanging in the window of a pet shop. "Money will buy a fine dog, but only love will make him wag his tail."

It really does work wonders.

When love is in charge you'll find it easy to keep the Golden Rule.

During a Sunday school class in Philadelphia the children were asked to write their favorite biblical truth on the blackboard. One girl wrote: "DO ONE TO OTHERS AS OTHERS DO ONE TO YOU."

I'm afraid she's been watching older folks too carefully. She's met the people who quote it, "Do unto others as they would do unto you—if they had a chance."

That's not it at all! The object is to give of yourself to somebody else.

God told it to Moses. Christ quoted it and Paul repeats it again, "For the whole Law is fulfilled in one word, in the statement, 'You shall love your neighbor as yourself' " (Galatians 5:14).

You aren't asked to love them *more* than yourself, or *less* than yourself, but *as* yourself. And that means you need to love yourself, too. It's mutual!

A Wedding in Miami

When Joyce Thomas announced her wedding to James DeBoard in Miami, she asked my wife and me to be in the wedding party.

We were honored. But then came the surprise. "By the way," said Joyce, "you'll have to memorize a song. I'm asking everyone on the platform to sing as a choir just after we exchange vows."

The song was the melody put to the words of "Eternal Life," by St. Francis of Assisi.

It was a moment no one present will forget as Joyce and James knelt and we sang:

> Lord, make me an instrument of your peace.
> Where there is hatred, let me sow love.
> Where there is injury, pardon.
> Where there is doubt, faith.
> Where there is despair, hope.
> Where there is darkness, light.
> And where there is sadness, joy.
> O Divine Master, grant that I may not so much seek
>   to be consoled as to console;
> To be understood as to understand;
> To be loved as to love.
> For it is in giving, that we receive.
> It is in pardoning that we are pardoned.
> And it is in dying that we are born to eternal life.

What a great way to begin a new life together. And what a lesson in love. Yes it *is* in giving that we receive.

Start giving, today.

THE CHOICE IS YOURS

We've been talking about the Ten Commandments, the "new" commandment, and the "greatest" commandment, but there's another that puts it all in focus. "And this is His commandment, that we believe in the name of His Son Jesus Christ, and love one another, just as He commanded us" (1 John 3:23).

Even though it is a command, we have the choice to accept or reject. And that's the way it is with love. We can elect to receive it, or we can say "No."

The final decision is yours!

Sometimes, however, we are faced with choices that seem impossible. Choices between law and love.

In Benjamin Franklin's autobiography is the account of an English clergyman who was ordered to read a special proclamation issued by King Charles I, which encouraged the people to return to participating in sports on Sunday.

Most church leaders refused to read the edict. But to the congregation's amazement, their minister read it. But he followed the pronouncement with the words, "Remember the Sabbath day to keep it holy." And he added, "Brethren, I have laid before you the commandment of your king and the commandment of your God. I leave it to you to judge which of the two ought to be observed."

Every day you are confronted with choices, options, and decisions. And you need to *let love become part of the process*.

The Best Present

Last Christmas a judge in Los Angeles listened as a young father who was arrested for stealing groceries cried and told him, "I can't find work and my children were hungry. That's why I did it."

The judge fined him $50. But the next day the same judge and his wife drove to the home of the family with two boxes filled with groceries and explained, "Young

122

man, as a judge I had an obligation to fine you in court, but as a man I want to help you have a Merry Christmas."

And that wasn't the end of the story. The judge helped the fellow find work and inspired him to straighten out his life.

Sure, he applied the law. But more than that, *he let love rule*.

But let me contrast that with a conversation I had with a man pumping gas in Tulsa. In our brief conversation he said, "I'm an accountant for a bank. I'm moonlighting so I can buy my kids some better presents this Christmas."

As I drove away I thought, "How sad!" Instead of working four hours every night he could have been home with his kids. And that's the best present he could ever give them—*himself*.

It is impossible to place a value on your love. What we give from our hearts has a much greater worth than what we give from our wallets.

You can choose to impress the world with your contributions, or you can quietly give of your time, your talents, and yes, *yourself*.

The account of what will happen when the sheep are separated from the goats is worth looking at.

The Lord tells how he will say to those who inherit the kingdom, "For I was hungry, and you gave Me something to eat; I was thirsty, and you gave Me drink; I was a stranger, and you invited Me in; naked and you clothed Me; I was sick, and you visited Me; I was in prison, and you came to Me."

But those who entered the kingdom were quite surprised. "Lord, when did we see You hungry and feed You, or thirsty and give You drink? And when did we see You a stranger and invite You in, or naked and clothe You? And when did we see You sick or in prison and come to You?"

Here is the Lord's reply, ". . . Truly I say to you, to the extent that you did it to one of these brothers of Mine, even the least of them, you did it to Me" (Matthew 25:35-40).

Love Can Lift You, Too

Your most insignificant act of kindness doesn't go unnoticed. Your smallest gift of love may become the most valuable possession you'll ever own.

Go ahead and give that gift. And let your love be guided by a force greater than yourself. There is a higher power and it can be yours.

I remember watching a ship being raised in a lock on the St. Lawrence Seaway. The huge ship was lifted— not by its own power, but by water which was poured into the lock from a high water level. It came from *above*. And the huge seagoing vessel was lifted.

Your life can be filled with "living water" from above. And it will lift you to a new level. To a new life. To a new love.

Admiral Richard Byrd spent five isolated months in 1934 in a shack in the Antarctic recording scientific data. It was cold and bleak. But he wrote in his book *Alone*, "For those who seek it, there is inexhaustible evidence of an all-pervading intelligence."

For that reason, Byrd never really felt alone.

Love has hundreds of attributes, but Paul summed it up when he said, "Love never fails. . ." (1 Corinthians 13:8). It lasts!

What a transformation when the Yes Yes living of the new commandment fulfills the laws of a No No world.

One word did it. *Love!*

It's going to change your world, too.

9

Great Expectations!

Little Billy's mother asked him to help her by filling a pan with apples.

He brought it to her and said, "It's full. I can't get any more in it."

His mom thought she'd teach Billy a lesson and said, "It's not full at all." Then she added a quart of beans that fit between the cracks.

"Well, it sure is full now," said Billy.

"No, it's not."

She added a quart of wheat, two handfuls of flour, and two cups of water. Then she smiled at her son and said, "Now, it's full!"

Just when you think you're too busy. Just when you think your life is too full. Remember, *there is room for much more.*

Don't sell tomorrow short. Your future is as great as your foresight. And there's plenty to get excited about.

Yes Yes living is filled with anticipation, with hope

and with confidence. It is filled with great expectations.

"He always believes something good is going to happen." That's what they'll say about you when positive predictions are all you know.

What is on your horizon? What are you expecting to happen?

HOPING FOR THE BEST

Everybody likes a bonus. And when you exceed their expectations, you're a winner.

Let me tell you what happened in New York City.

Two almost identical candy booths are located at each end of the lobby of a large office building. About the same number of people pass each booth, they sell identical candies, and are managed by two equally pleasant girls. Yet one always has twice as many customers as the other.

What is the magic formula? The more successful girl shared her secret.

"It's all in the scooping," she said. "A normal scoop puts too much candy on the scales. That means you have to take some away, and the customer feels cheated."

She explained, "I'm always careful to scoop too little the first time and then add a little more. The customer feels like he is getting a bonus. It's amazing how business has increased."

Think about it! When the candy was taken away, business slumped, but when it was added, sales soared. That's what happens when expectations are exceeded.

Everybody wants that "little extra" and you can give it to them. Get in the habit of presenting pearls instead of peanuts. Give them *more* than they expect.

What does your family expect from you? Give them *more*. What does your employer expect of you? Give him *more*. What about your community? What about your church?

It's the same in life as it is in the Olympics. The winners are those who give just a little bit more. Just 1/100 of a second can mean the difference between a Gold Medal or second place.

You say, "But the more I give, the more I am expected to give." That's true. And it is the best possible position to be in.

When someone expects more from you than you expect from yourself, something exciting happens. It's like shifting gears. You reach a new level of accomplishment.

Ringing the Bell

Something happened to me one day on a lecture tour that proved the power of expectation.

I was in Wisconsin on a tour for the School Assembly Service, speaking to about three high-school audiences every day. Some groups were lively, others were dull. One hour I felt as though I had rung the bell. The next hour I wished the bell would ring.

How could crowd reaction be so varied? Was it the time of day? Was it the volume level of the microphone? Was it the temperature in the auditorium? The lighting? I just couldn't figure it out.

Then one morning in a school near Madison, I had what I still consider to be the roughest speaking experience of my life.

The principal was out of town. The noisy students filled the auditorium. There was obviously no teacher supervision.

Finally, a student I had not met walked out to the podium and said, "OK, you guys. Let's get quiet. We've got a speaker here today. I don't know his name so I'll just turn it to him."

Wow! I was in shock. No introduction. No applause. They didn't even *hear* him when he told them to be quiet.

Somehow I managed to get their attention and survived the hour.

But that same afternoon, at a school less than ten miles away, I had an introduction that was every bit as surprising.

The principal stood before the assembled students and began by saying, "Today we have with us one of the most outstanding speakers you will ever have the privilege of hearing."

Was I in the right school?

He went on for about three minutes with glowing statements that exaggerated my background beyond belief. All of a sudden I had awards and honors I'd never heard of.

He concluded with, "Please join me in welcoming our speaker, Neil Eskelin." I walked out to a standing, cheering student body.

I thought, "Should I tell them the principal

stretched the truth? Should I explain the exaggeration?"

No. They expected a great speaker and I wasn't going to let them down. For nearly one hour I delivered that speech in an "electric" atmosphere. I caught myself listening as though someone else was talking through me. It was an indescribable experience.

What a shocking difference between an audience with _no_ expectation and one with *great* expectation.

You'll never know what you are capable of until you find yourself living up to expectations greater than your own.

Don't be afraid to take a giant step up. If someone believes you can do it, you'd better give it a try. You'll be astonished at your own accomplishments.

Let the power of expectation work for you. When you hope for the best, you'll deliver the best—*and even more.*

TELL ME WHAT YOU EXPECT

Last week a college student was in my office and I asked him, "What are you going to be doing ten years from today?"

He thought about it and said, "Really, I don't have the slightest idea."

I've asked that question to hundreds of teens and college youth and nine out of ten have no specific answer. If they do, their answer usually begins with, "I might," "Perhaps," or "Maybe."

If you can tell me your goals, plans and specific expectations, you're much closer to reaching them than you know.

Just *stating* them is a great start. And as one of my teachers used to say, "Beginning is half done."

Yes, you're halfway there. Think about it! When you say, "I don't know what I'll be doing, you're halfway to nowhere. And when you say "I can't," you're halfway to failure.

Every time you describe your tomorrow in terms of anxiety, alarm, or despair, you set in motion the very thing you are trying to escape. And that is how the No No World stays in business.

Believe It and You'll See It

Do you remember the story of Job? He lost his health, his family, and all his possessions, and he said, "For what I fear comes upon me, and what I dread befalls me" (Job 3:25).

Yes, the law of Asking and Receiving applies to both good and bad. If you look for failure you're sure to find it.

It's like the young convert of John Wesley who had been sent up to the North of England to preach. After a year he returned to Wesley searching for the reason his preaching did not produce more converts.

Wesley asked, "You don't expect to have converts at every meeting, do you?"

"Oh, no!" said the young preacher, "not at *every* meeting."

Wesley replied, "Then that's the reason you aren't having more of them."

Some folks go through life with the motto: "Seeing is

believing." They've got to "touch" it before they say it is true. But the sign on the road to Yes Yes living reads, "Believe it and you'll see it."

Expect the extraordinary and it will be yours.

Nancy Androtti teaches ninth-grade social studies at a high school in Brooklyn. It is not a paradise. Teachers and students have been mugged and even raped in the building. Armed guards are on duty and faculty turnover is high.

But Nancy, a twenty-eight-year-old, has not once been threatened or harassed. In fact, the students would fight *for* her if it ever came to that.

In a workshop for teachers on discipline, she said, "During the first week of every semester, I don't teach. Instead, I sit down with every student individually and ask them about their families, their friends, their interests, and their hopes for the future."

Then she tells each one, "I have great expectations of you this semester and I know you won't let me down."

They don't.

Nancy communicates total respect, concern, and love for her students. She doesn't *demand* a positive teaching environment, she just expects it, and it happens.

People respond to respect. And they don't want to disappoint your expectations. When you demonstrate a positive belief, you'll see positive behavior.

His Behavior Changed

A lady who has spent a number of years working with delinquent girls told me of a rather frightening experience she had with a man who tried to physically abuse her because she had tried to help a young girl he obviously disliked.

I asked, "How were you able to stop him?"

"It was easy," she said. "I just told him, 'I'm sure you were raised to have good manners!' "

The message got through, and he quit. Her expectations changed his abusive behavior.

When you *believe* the situation will be solved, everything you say and do reflects that faith in such a way that it *does* happen.

If you really *expect* a project to succeed, every action related to that goal will serve to insure its success. On the other hand, when you fear it will fold, you'll dwell on the weakest link in the chain until it breaks.

Thinking great thoughts and expecting great results only get you started in the right direction. *Doing something about it* is what really matters.

You can expect your car to take you from home to your job, but nothing happens until you turn the ignition, put it in gear, push the accelerator and turn the wheel. That is what gets you somewhere.

What is it you expect? What are you doing to achieve it?

YOU GOTTA BELIEVE

"More people are humbugged into believing too little than are humbugged into believing too much." That's what the great showman P.T. Barnum said.

It's true that our expectations are low because our belief is shallow. And most people live by the philosophy that says, "If it hasn't happened to me, I don't believe it." Or, "If it isn't logical, I won't accept it."

One of the world's greatest myths is that there is a link between intelligence and success. Or, as you may have been asked, "If you're so smart, why aren't you rich?"

No, brain power doesn't guarantee the good life. In fact there are thousands of scientists, technologists, and mathematicians who would gladly trade a few points of their I.Q. for a Yes Yes approach to living.

They'd like to return to the simple act of believing.

Thinking doesn't produce hope.

Logic doesn't produce faith.

And your I.Q. doesn't produce the belief that tomorrow will be better than today.

These are the life-sustaining qualities that have closer links with "soul power" than with "mind power."

Inside Your Fortune Cookie

We enjoy taking our friends to a restaurant called Gee's East Wind. Great Chinese cooking. And the fun comes when the "fortunes" are pulled from those little cookies.

"A stranger will bring you good luck."

"Beware of business opportunity."

"Love is on your horizon."

And I'm still waiting for the one that reads, "Help, I am a prisoner in a Chinese cookie factory."

It is surprising, but some actually take those paper prophecies seriously. They apply the power of belief and expectation to almost anything and make little distinction between positive and negative forecasts.

Dr. James Kinser, a psychologist from Washington, D.C., told me, "I see people every day who are actually expecting the worst to happen. And in many cases, it is their expectation that is the real problem."

He quoted a few of his patients:

"I don't know what it is, but I know I've got a serious health condition."

"Financially, we're just not going to make it."

"I just don't know how this marriage is going to last."

You may create a facade of confidence, but it's purely cosmetic. The real you—*the person inside*—starts to show when you start to think about the future.

Whether you like it or not, expectancy is a dynamic force that is playing a great part in your life.

Who Determines Your Day?

Recently, I heard a speaker at the Rotary Club expound on the topic of "Biorhythms." And according to him, life is a series of three cycles. Physical, emotional, and intellectual. Each cycle has a different number of days.

His business was selling a computer printout (based on your birth date) that would show the "good" days and the "bad" days for each of the three factors. But as he told us, "The most dangerous of all days is when the cycles cross each other—and especially when all three cross on the same day."

My reaction was, "Who cares?"

Evidently, somebody does.

I returned to my office and was laughing about the topic to my secretary. But not for long.

Louella unfolded a printout and said, "I thought everybody knew about biorhythms. This is my chart."

Sure enough. Every day was plotted. She knew just what to expect.

"Louella," I said. "How can I believe that life fluctuates between positive and negative positions of a cycle when I maintain a Yes Yes attitude 98 percent of the time?" (I'm working on the other two percent.)

Why should I even listen to a prediction that I would have a bad day? I expect good things to happen, and they do.

Have you ever met an astrology addict? You say, "How are you?" And they reply with, "What's your sign?"

Their day is dictated by Jeanne Dixon.

What a yo-yo life! Up one day and down the next, depending on their personal horoscope.

You don't have to consult the signs of the zodiac to know what is about to happen.

To put it bluntly, you'll *never* know total Yes Yes living if you have the slightest belief in astrology.

Oh, the power of expectancy!

Forget what others think. It's time to bake your own fortune cookie!

Did Bruce Jenner look at a chart to see if he should enter the Montreal Olympics?

How often did Muhammad Ali predict he was going to lose?

Did Churchill say, "We *might* win?"

Of course not!

They charted their destiny by declarations of expectancy. Then they proved what they believed.

That is what true champions are made of. *You gotta believe.*

I CAN'T WAIT FOR TOMORROW

A few weeks ago I was having lunch with two businessmen and one was an outspoken critic of anything related to positive attitude.

He said, "I used to get up in the morning and say, 'Wow! This is going to be the best day of my life!' But sometimes it didn't work. So I quit. Now I just take whatever comes."

It was obvious.

His contribution to the conversation was to tell us what was wrong with the government, how inflation was going to bankrupt his business, and how those pains in his back seemed to be getting worse.

He was filled with expectation all right—but the wrong kind.

Certainly you will have setbacks, trials, delays and unpleasant circumstances, but they should not alter your basic philosophy of living. In the long run, things are going to get better. *Much* better.

A stockbroker for Merrill Lynch told me, "The investor who is worried about tomorrow goes broke playing the market. I've seen plenty of investors take huge losses on stocks because they had no faith the price would ever bounce back."

Then he told me, "The guy who has faith in the

future will wind up rich because he is consistent. He buys when it's high and he buys when it's low. Over the long haul he accumulates large quantities of stock and the value is enormous."

He added, "It takes a certain *type* to make it in the market. He's got to believe in the future."

Yes, you've got to believe that today is *good*, tomorrow is *better*, and that the day after tomorrow will be the *best*.

It's been said that "There is no such thing as a hopeless situation. Only hopeless people."

Tomorrow *is* going to be better.

Soybean Pancakes for Lunch

During the spring of 1961 it was time for me to get serious about landing a good job. I was finishing an M.A. in broadcast communications from Ohio State University and I listened to some good offers from the networks, ad agencies, and audience research bureaus. They sounded attractive, but I just knew something better would come along.

In July, I was attending a convention in Miami Beach and met a fellow who shared his vision with me about what broadcasting *could* be in this country.

Then he said, "Neil, I'm just getting started and I'd like you to be the first full-time employee."

I didn't want to sound too mercenary, but I finally asked, "What would the salary be?"

He said, "We can pay you $40 per week."

I thought he was joking, but he was dead serious. I told him, "I'll think about it," and that was that.

Forty dollars a week when I'd been offered the moon in Manhattan? I'd have to be crazy to accept it.

I was!

Three days later I got on a train and traveled several hundred miles up the Atlantic coast to the home of the man I met in Miami. And when I arrived I was in for a greater shock than I imagined.

The family was living near the edge of starvation. We had soybean pancakes for lunch.

Then he took me to my office. It was a run-down UHF television station that was off the air because there were no TV sets manufactured with UHF in 1961. It took an expensive "converter" to pull in the signal.

Vandals had broken the tubes. The transmitter didn't work. Dogs and cats had littered the floor.

He told me, "Neil, I know I told you we could pay you $40 a week, but we just don't have it." Then he smiled and said, "But you can have any title you want: program director, producer, you name it."

The Future Was Today

The money or the title didn't matter. I sensed immediately that this was going to be much more than a job.

I was living with Pat and Dede Robertson and we were about to launch the Christian Broadcasting Network with the world's first religious television station, WYAH-TV, in Portsmouth, Virginia.

Yes, we were working in a run-down studio, with broken tubes, and one old black-and-white RCA TV camera. But we saw something far greater.

Even before October 1, 1961, when by a miracle the FCC allowed us to hit the air, we saw a great network broadcasting wholesome TV programs. We saw international affiliates. We talked about the day when satellites would carry the programs to thousands of cities.

That's what made us work sixteen hours a day without even thinking about it.

We saw the future as if it were today. Perhaps you've read the whole story in the bestseller, *Shout It From the Housetops* (Logos).

On October 1, 1979, eighteen years later, Pat and I talked about those days on "The 700 Club," CBN's anchor program. But now we were standing in a $30 million television facility that turns commercial broadcasters green with envy. And now we were communicating with millions of people around the globe.

When the tapes stopped rolling, Pat turned to me and said, "Neil, I'm so excited about what is about to happen. The opportunities we have are incredible."

The same sense of anticipation remained. The vision was still there! Yes, today was great, but just wait until tomorrow!

Is that the way you feel about it? Are you filled with hope and excitement about tomorrow?

I'm asking you to see things not as they are, but *as they are going to be.* See your family not as they are, but *as they are going to be.* See yourself, not as you are, but *as you are going to be.*

It's true. "Greater things shall ye do."

Why not start today?

10

The Amazing Power of Encouragement!

When Barry showed up at his Boy Scout troop meeting with a black eye, his scoutmaster was concerned.

"What happened?"

Barry told how he tried to help a little old lady across the street.

"How in the world could you get a black eye doing that?" asked the scoutmaster.

Barry smiled and said, "She didn't want to go!"

Not everybody wants your help, but most people do. Not everybody will respond to your encouragement, but it will make a difference in the lives of those you touch. It will make a difference in your life, too.

Something extraordinary happens when you join forces with someone else. What seems impossible for you to do alone is suddenly simple when tackled by a "team."

We're going to talk about the amazing power of encouragement. You'll see how it works in reaching goals, in building businesses, in making friends, and in self-motivation. You'll see how it works for *you*.

Turn your back on the No No world that wants you to "go it alone." We need each other now more than ever before. Together, there's no telling what can be accomplished.

HELP IS ON THE WAY

"Premiums" have become a big part of the business world. In fact an entire industry has been built around the incentives offered to encourage productivity.

The top appliance salesman gets a trip to Bermuda. The leading store manager gets a new car. If you add to your savings account, you'll get a set of cookware.

It works! *We love to be encouraged.*

An employee of Sears, Roebuck and Co., told me how much the former president of the firm, Robert Elkton Wood, believed in incentives. Wood tried the technique in his own family.

He really wanted to have a lot of grandchildren. So he told each of his four daughters, "I'll give you a mink coat at the birth of your third child."

Wood had *fifteen* grandchildren! *Now that's productivity!*

You are using premiums and incentives, too. Every day you make promises designed to encourage people to behave exactly as you want them to.

But instead of encouraging, most of our promises *discourage*.

"If you're not back by suppertime, you can't use the car this weekend!"

"Either finish your reading assignment or you're going to fail this course!"

"You'd better sell at least three houses this month or find a new real estate company to represent."

Are you using incentives or are you using threats? Successful premiums are almost always *positive*. Try trading something *you* want for something *they* want and watch what happens.

Share the Reward

At the age of sixteen, a farm boy began to tell his mother of his dream to start a business of his own. He was barely literate, but his mother wanted to encourage him any way she could.

She loaned him $100 and he bought a little boat. He started a "rain-or-shine" ferry service from Staten Island, where he lived, to Manhattan.

At the end of the first year he gave an envelope to his mother. It contained $1,100 and a note thanking her for helping him in the new venture.

The business grew into shipping and railroads. Cornelius Vanderbilt multiplied his mother's $100 by millions and millions. But it all started with some heartfelt encouragement.

You're only going to live once. *Don't waste your years saying "No" to those you have a chance to help*. Instead, join them in their effort and you'll *both* share in the reward.

Even if the goal is never reached, there is a great joy in knowing that you tried—*together*.

But so often we create barriers that separate us from the people we are trying to help. It's like trying to run a world relief agency from a posh penthouse in Philadelphia. It won't work!

When John Patterson took over the National Cash Register company, guess where he put his office? *Right in the middle of the factory floor*. His goal was to create an atmosphere that encouraged productivity. And he decided the best place to be was right there with the employees.

It worked! NCR grew enormously under Patterson's leadership. And he was in the middle of it all.

It's time to come down from that ivory tower. *It's time to break the barrier that separates you from those you can really help.*

We are *one!* And we need to start practicing it. Like the sign I saw in the gift shop at JFK International Airport, "One language builds a fence. Two languages can construct a gate."

It's true in the world. And it's true at home. *We really do need each other!*

"Reach Out and Touch Someone"

Just look at what the Word says. "*Comfort* one another . . . *bear* one another's burdens . . . *edify* one another . . . *pray* one for another . . . *forgive* one another . . . *love* one another." And here's what happens when we do: ". . . if we love one another, God abides in us, and His love is perfected in us" (1 John 4:12).

I can still hear the little song the Bell Telephone Company uses in its commercial, "Reach out. Reach out and touch someone. Reach out. Reach out and just say 'Hi!' "

It's so important to seize the opportunity to touch someone's life. You may never have the chance again.

After giving an address to the Ft. Lauderdale, Florida, Chamber of Commerce, a young man waited until the crowd had dwindled and asked if he could speak with me.

The topic of my talk that day was "Give It All You've Got!" and I had touched on the importance of "giving yourself completely to someone else."

He said, "My name is Dave and I'm a salesman for a computer company." He continued, "I almost didn't come today because I've been ready to quit my job. But there's something you said that struck me like a bolt of lightning.

"You said, 'The five most important words in any conversation are: How can I help you?' And I realized that my attitude has been exactly the opposite."

He confessed that his entire approach had been based on what his customers could do for *him*. He said, "Even before I walk in to sell to a new customer I think about the particular computer I'd like to sell."

Dave said, "I realize that it's all *my* needs, *my* plans, and *my* goals."

He left determined to *do* something for his customers rather than to sell them something.

Well, I've never heard how he fared, but I was convinced that his business would increase. It *always* does when you *put people ahead of products*.

Try using those five magic words: "HOW CAN I HELP YOU?" Go ahead and start helping!

WE'RE IN THIS THING TOGETHER

One of the most spectacular mountain climbs on record was the assault on Mt. Everest by Edmund Hillary and his native guide, Tenzing.

While they were descending from that forbidding peak, Hillary suddenly lost his footing. But Tenzing instantly dug his axe into the ice, held the rope taut and kept both of them from falling.

When they were interviewed by newsmen, Tenzing refused any special credit for saving Hillary's life. He said it was just a normal, routine part of his job. And he added, "Mountain climbers *always* help each other."

But you don't have to be on a mountain to find people who need your assistance. Just look around and you'll find people who are waiting for you to say, "Yes, I'll help!"

Let me say it again. We *do* need each other. Just as one part of your body needs the other parts of your body to make it function, God didn't create man to be alone. Yes, we're in this thing together!

Every person you meet can have special value to your life—if you'll just let them. It's so easy to see the thousands and forget they are all unique individuals.

Yes, even *one* is worth your attention.

An Audience of One

In Louisiana, however, they told me about a young politician who almost overdid it.

When he arrived at the auditorium for his first campaign speech, there was only one man in the audience. And when he finally realized that no one else was going

148

to show up, he walked over to the man and said, "Mister, I'm just a young politician starting out. Do you think I ought to deliver this speech or should I dismiss this meeting?"

The fellow thought for a moment and said, "Well, sir, I'm just a cowhand. All I really know is about cows. But I do know that if I took a load of hay down to the pasture and only one cow came up, I'd feed it."

The young candidate took his advice and started his speech. He talked for an hour and a half. But the cowhand didn't say a word. He just listened.

When it was over, the politician said, "Well, that's it. Was my speech all right?"

The man smiled and said, "Like I said, sir. All I know is about cows. But I do know if I took a load of hay down to the pasture and only one cow came up, I'll be hanged if I'd give her the whole load."

Well, you've got to give him credit for trying. And the cowhand certainly gave him plenty of encouragement.

But whether you deliver the "whole load" or just a handful, the important fact is that you give *something*. When people meet you, they should not go away empty-handed. Say it again and again, to everyone you possibly can, *"How can I help you?"*

Even when you think your help isn't wanted, *it usually is*. But some folks have a strange way of expressing it.

Very Close Encounters

A prof from the University of Minnesota who has taught for years told a group of novice teachers, "You'll discover that in every class there will be a student quite anxious to argue. Your first reaction will be to silence him. But my advice to you is to go slow. He is probably the only student in your class who is listening, and he needs your encouragement, not your scolding."

Again, "How can you help him?" If your goal is to teach, and his is to learn, remember—you're in this thing together.

Your life isn't isolated. The investment broker needs the services of the garbage collector—who needs the services of the physician—who needs the help of the tax consultant—who needs the services of the bank manager—and the circle never ends.

Studies have shown that we come in direct contact in person or by phone with nearly 100 people every day. Yes, you *do* have a great opportunity to influence so many lives. Make those moments count. *Start helping today.*

YOU'RE ALL RIGHT!

Everybody likes a little praise. And those who give it are the real heroes in life.

Have you ever seen a monument built to a critic? I doubt that you can find one. But there are statues everywhere honoring men and women who were distinguished as leaders. And if you'll take a close look at leaders from Abe Lincoln to Florence Nightingale, you'll find they not only received praise—they *gave* it.

In the life of every person you meet, there is some quality worth your acknowledgment.

Here's what happened to a newspaper cartoonist who

sent a mail-gram to twenty of his acquaintances. Each message was the same and it contained only one word, "Congratulations!"

But as far as he knew, not one of them had accomplished anything in particular worth congratulating.

Within two weeks he had a letter or a phone call of thanks from everyone on the list. And every one of them mentioned something they had done that seemed deserving of praise.

Most of them said, "I was really surprised you found out."

Yes, *everyone likes to be complimented.*

Join Dr. Crane's Club

During your lifetime there will be some brief encounters that will make a lasting impression on your life. Meeting George Crane was one of those special encounters for me.

I heard Dr. Crane, author of the syndicated newspaper column, *The Worry Clinic*, speak when I was just a teenager. After the lecture, our family was introduced to him.

During the conversation he told us about the old Chicago streetcar he had converted into a summer home on his farm near Hillsboro, Indiana. He invited us to visit and the following July we spent a memorable day with this extraordinary man and his family. (His sons, Daniel and Philip, became U.S. Congressmen.)

That afternoon he told us about one of his favorite projects, "The Compliment Club." He said, "It's really very simple. Several years ago I decided to single out three people every day and give them a sincere compliment." He said, "I might thank the grocery clerk for being so courteous. I may tell a salesman he had a great smile. I've even complimented the church custodian."

That simple idea has stayed with me to this day. I joined the "club" and look for people who deserve a "thank you" or a compliment.

It's a great encouragement—*for them*, and *for me*.

Why not join the "Compliment Club" yourself? Try it for just one day and watch what happens. *It's a sure-fire way to eliminate No No thinking.*

When your goal is to search for something worth praising, you just don't have time to dwell on those things you now find irritating.

Try it!

Why Mr. "No No" Fails

In business everyone is trying to climb a little higher on the ladder. But many fall off without realizing why.

Let's see what happens when someone wants the boss's job.

Here's how Mr. No No tries to get promoted. He attempts to get his boss fired by lying to the company president. He tries to discredit his superior to his peers. But it usually backfires and results in either a transfer or a demotion.

But Mr. Yes Yes has an entirely different approach. He is only thinking one thought: "How can I help my boss get a promotion?" He does everything within his power to praise his immediate superior because he knows that when the *boss* moves up, he will likely move up, too.

What is your approach? Can you see what is happening? Or is something blocking your vision?

Do you remember what Christ said on the mountain? ". . . why do you look at the speck in your brother's eye, but do not notice the log that is in your own eye? Or how can you say to your brother, 'Let me take the speck out of your eye,' and behold, the log is in your own eye?"

He called them "hypocrites," and said, ". . . first take the log out of your own eye, and then you will see clearly enough to take the speck out of your brother's eye" (Matthew 7:3-5).

Start seeing what is good. Instead of finding fault, you'll find favor.

ONE PLUS ONE IS MORE THAN TWO

New ideas are hard to sell when you're doing the job alone. But watch what happens when you get a little help.

In the early thirties, Robert Garst, from the big city of Coon Rapids, Iowa, traveled thousands of miles trying to sell a new hybrid corn to farmers.

The new corn, developed by Henry A. Wallace, a former U.S. vice president and farm magazine publisher, met with great resistance. Farmers had planted the same kind of corn for generations and Garst soon learned they weren't ready for a change. They told him, "We're not going to waste our money on that."

But he felt the hybrid corn would start a revolution if he could just get it started.

In desperation he decided if he couldn't sell it, he'd

give it away. So Garst packed as much of the corn as he could in seven-pound bags and gave it free to any farmer who would promise to plant it.

Those trial plots broke tradition and those farmers became his greatest sales team. They were sold on the product and Garst was on his way to amassing a fortune that was recently estimated at over $50 million.

One acre became one thousand. Ten thousand became 100 thousand and the success story grew beyond his fondest dreams.

When you form a "team," your efforts multiply dramatically.

A Mule Named "Pete"

We all have times when we are inspired by an idea. Or we have a plan that we just know will take the world by storm. But what happens when you share that dream? What is the reaction when you tell someone about your vision?

"It will never work."

"I know a fellow who tried that and went broke."

"That's the craziest thing I've ever heard of."

Why do they say it? Why do most people try to stick a pin in your balloon? *It's our No No nature.* When we say, "Don't try it," we are just getting ready for the time when we can say, "I told you so," or "You should have listened to me." Evidently, that makes a lot of people feel good.

But if you really want to feel great, try giving someone your encouragement. When they share their new idea, say "I'm behind you all the way," or "I know you can do it." They'll love you for it.

I need encouragement and you do, too. *Everybody does.*

Let me tell you about a farmer who had a mule. Every day he stood at the side of the field and hollered at him. "Get up Kate!" "Get up Will!" "Get up Sam!" He called him all kinds of names.

Finally, his curious neighbor walked over one morning and asked, "Why do you stand here every day calling your mule by all those names? What *is* his name, anyway?"

"Oh! His name is Pete."

"Then why don't you call him Pete?" asked the neighbor.

"Can't you see? I've got blinders on him and I've got him hooked up to a two-horse plow! He thinks he has help and he's doing twice the job! Just watch him!"

Think about it! When we even *imagine* somebody is helping, we work harder than ever. And when we *do* have help, it multiplies even more.

The Power of "Two"

What does it say in Deuteronomy 32:30? One shall chase "a thousand." But two shall put how many to flight? ". . . ten thousand."

Yes, one plus one *is* more than two.

Is it any wonder that Christ said, "If two of you agree on earth about anything that they may ask, it shall be done. . . . For where two or three have gathered together in My name, I am in their midst" (Matthew 18:19-20)?

You need the strength that only comes when you get together. "Two are better than one. . . . For if either of them falls, the other will lift up his companion. But woe to the one who falls when there is not another to lift him up" (Ecclesiastes 4:9-10).

The word "encourage" comes from the French word for *heart*. And that must be the source of your encouragement, too.

Oh, there's a place for strong words and stern actions, but they must come from a heart that really cares. As the German poet, Goethe, said, "Correction does much, but encouragement does more. Encouragement after censure is as the sun after a shower."

Right now, declare that you will begin to reach out in love to those who need you. Widen your circle and *embrace someone whose life will be changed because you care.*

Remember:

- We are *one*. Start practicing it.
- "Comfort one another."
- Put people ahead of products.
- Ask "How can I help you?"
- There's something in everyone worth praising.
- Value every person you meet.
- Join the "Compliment Club."
- When you join forces, the results multiply.

Join forces! *Let the amazing power of encouragement begin to work for you!*

11

The Secret Yes Yes Ingredient!

Let me tell you about two frogs who jumped into a bucket of cream on a dairy farm in Wisconsin.

"May as well give up," croaked one after trying in vain to get out. "We're gonners!"

"Keep on paddling," said the other frog. "We'll get out of this mess somehow!"

"It's no use," said the first. "Too thick to swim. Too thin to jump. Too slippery to crawl. We're bound to die sometime anyway, so it may as well be tonight." He sank to the bottom of the bucket and died.

His friend just kept on paddling, and paddling, and paddling. And by morning he was perched on a mass of butter which he churned all by himself. There he was, with a grin on his face, eating the flies that came swarming from every direction.

That little frog had discovered what most folks ignore. *If you stick with the task long enough, you're going to be a winner*.

He discovered the secret Yes Yes ingredient—*persistence*!

The frog is in great company. Martin Luther, Patrick Henry, and Babe Ruth fought the same odds. And it is still happening today!

The road you travel may be ice-covered. The hill you are climbing may seem too steep. The barriers you face may be made of steel. But remember, Mt. Everest wasn't conquered on the first attempt. The walls of Jericho didn't fall on the first try.

Don't let your dream die! Don't give up on that goal! Just a little more effort and you're there. One more mile. One more minute. One more inch to victory!

You're going to make it!

IT'S NOT THE START THAT COUNTS

If you think that the "right" background is a guarantee of success, think again.

Napoleon ranked 42nd in his class at the Royal Military Academy in Paris, but where are the monuments to the other 41?

Patrick Henry was a failure as a farmer. He became a shopkeeper, but was such a poor businessman that he landed hopelessly in debt. But he turned to law and became a legend of the Revolutionary War.

Booker T. Washington was born a slave in Virginia, but became the most respected black educator of his day.

Just because you get off to a poor start, don't quit the race. Life isn't a 100-yard dash—it's a *marathon*. You've got plenty of time to recover from the obstacles you'll face along the way.

Whether it's in education, athletics, business or politics, your only limits are self-imposed. If somebody else can do it, *why not you?*

Right to the Top

When he was only fifteen years old, Ted O'Neil began spending his summers working on a large yacht in the Boston Harbor. And the first job he was given was to take a flag to the very top of the mainmast.

It looked impossible! He had never climbed that high before. And besides, there was hardly any footing on the way up.

He looked at the captain and asked, "Has anybody ever done that?"

"Of course they have," said his new boss.

Ted told the captain, "If anybody ever did it, I can do it!"

Yes, he carried the flag to the top and that phrase became his personal slogan for life.

The *Guinness Book of World Records* is packed with the feats of ordinary people doing extraordinary things. They made history because they believed "If someone else can do it—I can do it *better.*"

They became committed to a challenge and gave it everything they had. And those same qualities produce winners in every possible profession.

Phi Delta Kappan, the magazine for leaders in education, recently listed the two characteristics that were most conspicuous in those nominated for "Teacher-of-the-Year" awards.

First, "there is a nebulous quality called *dedication*."

Second, "the attribute of *energy*, which has been called the trademark of good teaching."

But dedication and energy produce a third quality— *determination*. And that's what makes the difference!

When you are totally dedicated to an idea and you give it all the energy you possess, "giving up" is out of the question. You'll stick with it regardless of what happens.

Anybody has the energy to get things started. But it takes determination to *keep* things going!

"I Still Believed in It"

Ken Taylor had an idea. He believed that the Bible could be much better understood if it were translated "thought by thought" rather than word by word.

He selected several chapters from the New Testament and wrote them in today's language. He became so excited and inspired by the project that he immediately shared the work with a major publisher.

To his shock, the manuscript was rejected. He tried another, and another. No one would even consider publishing such a "common" edition of the Bible.

But he believed in his concept so completely that he went to the bank and borrowed the funds to self-publish 2,000 copies. Then he persuaded several bookstores to take a few copies of his new volume, *Living Letters*.

It was more than four months before Taylor received his first reorder. The rest is history. Now, *The Living Bible* has sold over 25 million copies and has been translated into over 100 languages of the world.

Dr. Taylor said, "It seemed like a failure, but I still believed in it."

What about your own dreams? How much do you really believe in them? Enough to risk your future? Enough to risk your finances?

Remember, just about everybody will say "No" to your idea. And you'll have reams of reasons for quitting along the way. But it's the finish, not the start, that counts.

Yes, you're going to reach that goal.

INCH BY INCH IT'S A CINCH

The reason most ideas die in their infancy is because we're not prepared for the hard work it takes to make them grow. Anybody can say, "I've got a fantastic idea." But when you ask them later how it went, they usually say, "I just didn't have time."

Any idea can grow if you give it consistent, regular attention. It doesn't happen overnight.

What would happen right now if you walked into a physical fitness gym and tried to bench-press 400 pounds?

I think I know the answer.

But just ask any body builder for his secret of lifting heavy weights and he'll tell you, "You've got to start small and work at it regularly. Just add a little more weight each day. You'll get there."

There are limits, however. I remember as a boy, we had a small tree in the back yard and a neighbor told me, "If you'll jump over it every day as it grows, there's no telling how high you'll be able to jump some day."

It's too bad we moved from that house or I might have made the Olympics.

You've got to start somewhere and keep moving up.

How One Dollar Became One Million

Little David didn't start with Goliath. First it was a bear. Then it was a lion. No wonder he had such confidence in those five smooth stones and a slingshot.

He worked up by degrees.

How many people do you know who tell you, "I'm waiting for my ship to come in." Or, "Just wait till I make my first million." It doesn't happen and they just keep on waiting.

Becoming a millionaire is *easy. Anyone* can do it. I know that sounds like an impossible exaggeration, but let me tell you what I mean.

If you placed a dollar a day in a checking account it would take 2,740 years to save $1,000,000.

But if you place just one dollar every day in a savings account at eight percent interest, you would be worth, $1,000,000 in sixty-six years.

Is it worth the effort?

A huge tree doesn't tumble with one swing of the axe. You've got to keep on swinging. Time after time after time. It's a law of success.

And here's something else worth remembering: *The more you invest, the better your chances of a great return.* Make sure the odds are in your favor.

Yes, it is possible to increase your chances of success today.

It's like planting radishes. The instructions say, "Plant one inch apart. After seedlings appear, thin to three inches apart."

The first time I read that, I thought, "Why not just plant them three inches apart to begin with?"

But the philosophy of the farmer is the same as the successful salesman. You have to play the odds. Not all seeds sprout. Not all calls result in a sale.

One Hundred Calls a Day

A friend told me his experience selling encyclopedias to work his way through college.

"Every day I would make 100 calls to set up appointments. Twelve out of 100 would agree to see my demonstration. I would pick out the six that sounded the most promising. Three would let me in the door. And I would average one sale."

Then I asked, "Well, did you go back and call on the other good prospects?"

He said, "Oh, no! The next day I made 100 fresh calls and did it all over again."

He played the odds and it worked day after day. It also taught him discipline, self-reliance, and perseverance.

The same law applies to many areas of life.

Take job hunting, for example. The more interviews you have, the better your odds become. Some quit after three or four. But why not try 100?

George Eliot said it plainly, "If we want more roses, we must plant more trees."

Today, start planting.

Nothing is easy, and it isn't supposed to be. Persistence means hard work. As God told Adam, "By the sweat of your face you shall eat bread . . ." (Genesis 3:19).

Anything worth achieving is also worth your sacrifice. It's going to take a dedicated effort and untold hours of hard work. And if you get discouraged, remember the words of Isaiah, who says, "Because the Lord God helps me, I will not be dismayed; therefore, I have set my face like flint to do his will, and I know that I will triumph" (Isaiah 50:7 TLB).

Set your goal and start working at it. Day by day. Inch by inch. That's the sure way to win.

THE BOOK DOESN'T END HERE

A question I am often asked is, "How do you find time to write a book?" And my answer is that I don't *have* the time, I *take* the time.

Perhaps I should turn it around and ask, "How do you find time to watch a baseball game?" We take the time to do whatever it is we think is important.

But what would happen if I put my pen down at this very moment? After writing thousands and thousands of words, what if I decided to quit?

Well, you wouldn't be reading this book. And I wouldn't know the satisfaction of completing the project that I believe in.

But there are half-completed books collecting dust all over the world. There are half-completed houses that people live in for a lifetime. And there are half-completed lives that are wasting away because somebody gave up on a dream.

Don't quit now! Don't recite all of the reasons you can't get the job done. Just go ahead and *do it!*

Elbert Hubbard told the story of what happened when war broke out between Spain and the United States. It was urgent that the president get a message to the leader of the insurgents. His name was Garcia. He was known to be somewhere in the mountains of Cuba and no mail or telegraph could reach him.

Someone said, "There's a fellow by the name of Rowan who will find Garcia for you if anybody can."

Rowan took the letter without hesitation. He sealed it in a leather pouched strapped over his heart. He landed in the night off the coast of Cuba and made his way to the mountains and found Garcia.

He handed him the letter, turned around and headed home.

Hubbard's account of *A Letter to Garcia,* is an inspiration to those who value hard work. Rowan didn't ask, "Exactly where is he?" He didn't say, "I doubt if I can do it!"

He refused to complain. *There was a job to be done and he did it.*

Instead of making a dozen excuses of why you can't do the job, think about Rowan. Just go ahead and finish the task.

How Far is 10,000 Meters?

I remember the first time I tried jogging. My friends were telling me what a great exhilaration you get from the exercise.

Well, I tried it and ran out of breath in about three minutes. But the next day I tried it again, and the next. Finally, I was jogging about thirty minutes, three or four times a week.

Then a friend called and said, "There's going to be a 10,000-meter race next Saturday to raise money for the Cancer Society. Do you want to enter?"

In a weak moment I said, "Yes." The only problem was that I didn't know much about the metric system.

There must have been 150 runners out there. And I knew I was in trouble when I overheard two fellows talking about their experience running in the Boston Marathon. But the starting gun sounded and within two minutes I had the field to myself—nearly everybody else was way ahead of me.

I finally caught up to an old man who was running and asked, "Exactly how far is 10,000 meters anyway?" He said, "It's 6.2 miles." And right then I knew that the only race I was in was *the race with myself*.

I had never run that far before and it began to show. My feet were shouting, "Quit!" My legs were saying, "Give up!" My back was warning, "You'd better stop now!" And at the half-way point my wife gave me a look that said, "Are you all right?"

But the exhaustion and the pain just made me more determined than ever to cross the finish line. It took one hour and 16 seconds, but I made it.

You might say I've run *two* 10,000 meter races—*my first* and *my last*, but I haven't stopped jogging.

Completing that race was no different than finishing

any other task. You simply have to decide to reach the goal and take it *one step at a time.*

Giving up just won't do!

Martin Luther faced a world of pressure to abandon his cause. But rather than go against his conscience and do something he didn't feel was right, he exclaimed to the world: "If I had a thousand heads, I would lose them all rather than recant."

When you are determined to win, *quitting is out of the question.*

Babe Ruth led the league in strikeouts for five years, but that didn't keep him out of the Baseball Hall of Fame.

Have you made a commitment to stay in the race? Will you finish the task?

THE PRAYER OF PERSISTENCE

When it seems that the odds against you are too great and you hear those little voices telling you to "give in," that's the time for some Yes Yes resolve. It is also the time to pray.

Listen to the words of Admiral Chester Nimitz, who inspired the Pacific Fleet to victory over Japan. He prayed, "God grant me the courage to change the things I can change, the serenity to accept those I cannot change, and the wisdom to know the difference—but God grant me the courage not to give up on what I think is right even though I think it is hopeless."

What a prayer of persistence!

Yes, God *can* give you the courage to hold on to what

you believe is right. Ask Him to give you that courage today.

There's a question, however, that never stops being asked. "What is the secret of success?" Here's a nine word definition: "Stick to it! Stick to it! Stick to it!"

Edison did. Columbus did. Babe Ruth did. And today, you can too.

Was He a Failure?

The next time you consider giving up, think of the setbacks in the life of America's super statesman.

His business failed in 1831. He was defeated for the State Legislature in 1832 and failed again at business in 1833. The next year he was elected to the Legislature. Then his sweetheart died in 1835 and that was followed by a nervous breakdown.

Most of us would have called it quits. But he continued.

In 1838 he lost his bid for Speaker and was defeated for Elector in 1840. He was defeated for Congress in 1843. But he won the Congressional race in 1846 only to suffer defeat again in 1848. Then he was defeated for the Senate in 1858.

After all of this he was elected President of the United States in 1860. But we don't think about his failures. We remember Abraham Lincoln as a great President.

How would you react? Would you give up, or press on?

Today, when a problem appears, try to remember what happened to Lincoln.

Life is filled with challenges, choices, and even catastrophes. Millions fail once and never try again.

But Longfellow said, "Perseverance is a great element of success. If you only knock long enough and loud enough at the gate, you are sure to wake up somebody."

As Paul said it, ". . . one thing I do: forgetting what lies behind and reaching forward to what lies ahead. I press on toward the goal for the prize. . ." (Philippians 3:13,14).

Paul forgot those things of the past. He set his mind on a goal, a *right* goal, and he didn't let anything block his vision.

"Sail On"—No Matter What

Don't allow small, trivial annoyances to rob you of Yes Yes living. Set your sights on that special goal, and keep moving straight ahead.

It's like the grandfather who was walking along the beach with his grandson. The boy was telling him about the problems he was having at school.

"Grandpa, they're telling lies about me. They're trying to get me in all kinds of trouble."

The grandfather listened to the boy's troubles for a while. Then he reached down, took a handful of seaweed, and held it up to his grandson's eyes.

"Tell me. What do you see?"

The boy said, "Just some seaweed."

"Anything else?"

"No."

"Well, do you see that sailboat over there?"

"No."

"Why not?" asked the grandfather.

"Because you're holding that stuff too close to my eyes."

"That's exactly right!" he told the boy. "When the little things in life, like someone trying to hurt your feelings, get too close, you just can't see the things that are beautiful."

There are hundreds of things that will block your view. And there are storms that will take you off your course. But don't let anything stop your progress. Keep your ship headed in the right direction, and there's no telling what you'll discover.

To read the diary of Christopher Columbus at first seems quite repetitious.

"This day we sailed on."

Storms were buffeting the ships.

"This day we sailed on."

The *Pinta* was breaking apart.

"This day we sailed on."

There was hunger and darkness.

They sailed on!

Why not make that your motto? *Be determined to "sail on"—no matter what.*

We've been talking about one of the essential elements of Yes Yes living—persistence. It's a habit worth getting hooked on.

Ask yourself these questions:

If I fail in the first attempt, will I try again? Will I go the second mile—and the third?

If someone else has done it, can I do it too?

170

Will I do *more* than is necessary to reach my goal? Will I do something *every day* about it?

Will I make the required sacrifice to win the race?

Will I accept the task and complete it without complaining?

Do I ask for God's help?

Regardless of what happens, will I "sail on"?

If you can say "Yes," you'll join the mighty minority of life's real winners.

Like the frog in the bucket of cream. *Keep on paddling!*

12

Your Life Can Never Be the Same!

Right now, your life can take a turn for the best. You can make the decision to say goodbye forever to the No No world.

That's what I am asking you to do. Not next year. Not tomorrow. *You can begin today!*

It starts with a commitment to live the Yes Yes life. And it will affect everything you do.

Your circumstances will begin to brighten.

Your fears will fade.

Your words will have that "Yes Yes" ring.

Your action will be affirmative.

Your objectives will become attainable.

You'll see what love can do.

Your problems will shrink.

Your expectations will soar.

You'll suddenly have encouragement.

And you'll surely win because of your newfound persistence.

That's what we've been talking about. And now it's time to begin.

You say, "That's not me." "I'll lose my personality." Or, "No one will believe me if I start living like that."

You're exactly right! When you close the door on your No No world, people *should* say, "That's not the same person!" "I can hardly believe the change!"

And they'll love the new you!

Start your new life today!

YOU AIN'T SEEN NOTHIN' YET!

Do you remember seeing Menotti's warm Christmas opera, *Amahl and the Night Visitors?* The young beggar, Amahl, found it almost impossible to convince his mother that there were three kings standing at the door of their humble home.

She didn't believe it because *it had never happened before.* But the kings were *real*, and they were waiting for an invitation to come in.

Yes, there are kings and kingdoms waiting at your door. The gifts they bring are yours—but no one is going to force you to receive them. You have to open the door. You have to welcome them in. It's up to you!

It has been said, "God gives every bird its food, but he doesn't throw it in the nest."

The transformation of your life from "No" to "Go" may be gradual, or it may happen as a sudden shock. The most important factor is that *you must want that change to happen.* And you must be willing to do something about it.

"Shout it Out"

I recall a student named Walter who came to my office and asked, "Do you ever give private lessons in public speaking?"

Well, I hadn't, but when I listened to him I was ready to give it a try.

Walter told me, "To be honest, I am so frightened in front of an audience that I just freeze up. My voice turns to a whisper. And I know it sounds foolish, but I get physically ill at the thought of standing up before a group of people."

But during the conversation I discovered that his problem was more than a fear of public speaking. He was suffering from one of the most acute cases of an inferiority complex I'd ever seen. It affected his total life.

Every Monday afternoon, for the rest of the semester, Walter came in for his "class."

What an experience! But during the first session Walter learned that he really did have something to talk about. He told me of some things in his background that I was convinced would be helpful to someone else.

I told him, "You've got something worth talking about."

Walter had suffered through an operation due to heart disease at the age of ten. He knew more about heart trouble than anyone I'd ever met. And you could see his confidence growing as I told him so.

The next week I scheduled the session in the largest classroom on campus. I closed the door and sat in the back of the room, as far from Walter as I could get.

Then I said, "Walter, tell me the story again about the operation."

He began and I shouted, "I can't hear you!" He continued and I said, "Louder! Louder!" I had him begin again and again. Each time I urged him to "Shout it out!"

At the end of that second session he was already doing something he couldn't imagine. He had something worth saying, and he was delivering it with all the gusto of a powerful orator.

And that's the way you should approach the addition of Yes Yes living to your life. Don't be timid about it. *Immerse yourself totally!* Go ahead and *over*compensate.

Add Some "Umph"

It's much better to let the pendulum swing *all the way* since the force of the No No world will keep pulling from the other side.

It won't hurt to spend your time being "superpositive" for a while. That should be your deliberate approach. And before too long you'll find that the Yes Yes life will become your normal, everyday, "unconscious" behavior.

That's what happened to Walter. He released his voice, his imagination, and his anxiety by doing something he had never done before.

I saw him two years later and he said, "I've never forgotten those 'shouting' sessions. It got me over my fear of people." He was now the camp director of a large youth retreat near San Bernardino, California.

For Walter, it was a personal triumph. And as a Georgia politician said, "Triumph is just *'umph'* added to *try.*"

Yes Yes living will start to add "umph" to your life. And that will be just the beginning!

It's like the Washington, D.C., taxi driver who had a passenger from Ft. Smith, Arkansas. They passed the National Archives Building and the tourist saw the words carved in stone, "What Is Past Is Prologue."

"What in the world does that mean?"

The cab driver said, "It means that *you ain't seen nothin' yet!*"

As Eliphaz told Job, "You will . . . decree a thing, and it will be established for you; And light will shine on your ways" (Job 22:28).

And listen to the words of Paul as he quoted Isaiah: "Eye hath not seen, nor ear heard, neither have entered into the heart of man, the things which God hath prepared for them that love him" (1 Corinthians 2:9 KJV).

That's right! You ain't seen nothin' yet!

IT'S ABOUT TIME

But the clock on the wall keeps moving. And the best time to begin is *now.*

When the Airline Deregulation Act of 1978 was signed, it permitted airlines to apply on a first-come, first-served basis for any of the 1,300-plus dormant routes the Civil Aeronautics Board had previously awarded, but no carriers were currently serving.

Braniff International immediately snapped up 437 routes.

"I'm in a big hurry," said Harding Lawrence, the 58-year-old chairman and chief executive officer. "I don't have much time left to do what I want to do with this airline."

Whatever it is you plan to accomplish. Whatever your goals might be, *get busy! Start today!*

I heard about the advice Sir William Osler gave the students at Yale: "Live neither in the past nor in the future, but let each day's work absorb all your interest, energy, and enthusiasm. The best preparation for tomorrow is to do today's work superbly well."

Have you stopped crying about the past? Are you finished with your regrets about yesterday? It's time to close the history book and start to write today's chronicle.

As Dr. Frederick Loomis put it, "It's but little good you'll do, watering last year's crops."

And just as vital is the question, "Have you stopped worrying about the future?" *Have you erased the fear of tomorrow?*

The Time Trap

Remember what Christ said on the mountain, "Do not be anxious for your life, as to what you shall eat, or what you shall drink; nor for your body, as to what you shall put on. Is not life more than food, and the body more than clothing?

"Look at the birds of the air, that they do not sow, neither do they reap, nor gather into barns, and yet your heavenly Father feeds them. Are you not worth much more than they?"

Then He concludes by saying, "Therefore do not be anxious for tomorrow; for tomorrow will care for itself . . ." (Matthew 6:25, 26, 34).

It can't be emphasized enough. If you're caught between the failures of yesterday and the fears of tomorrow, it's like standing in the center of a giant vise. The sides will slowly come together and there's no more room. *You're trapped!*

But it doesn't have to happen! The slate of your past can be wiped clean. And you know who holds the future. So you're left with the most important time of all—*today.*

You don't have to "find" time. You don't have to search for it. It's simply there—every day. Twenty-four hours of it. And it is a gift that is given equally to presidents and paupers.

Yes, it's *yours.* To squander or to save. To use wisely or to throw away.

You Only Have a Minute

Horace Mann wrote the greatest classified ad of all time when he penned these words:

> Lost: Somewhere between sunrise and sunset, two golden hours, each set with sixty diamond minutes. No reward is offered for they are gone forever.

Think for just a moment about the goal you have in mind. Think about your special objective. When will you reach it? What must be done? And when will you do it?

There's only one answer. You've got to do something about it *today!* Yes, this very hour.

Tomorrow is nothing more than a series of *todays*. Don't waste them with idle dreams. Every minute counts.

A salesman in St. Paul handed me his card. On the back were these words:

> I have only just a minute.
> Only sixty seconds in it.
> Didn't seek it, didn't choose it.
> But it's up to me to use it.
> I must suffer if I lose it.
> Give account if I abuse it.
> Just a tiny little minute.
> But Eternity is in it.

Think of the responsibility! But more important, think of the *opportunity!* A minute doesn't sound like much, but it has value beyond measure.

To an advertiser, it's all the time he has to tell people about his product. To an auto racer it means the difference between victory and defeat. To a surgeon it means the time between life and death.

Just one minute. It's more important than we think.

As someone bluntly put it, "The Lord gave you two ends—one for sitting and one for thinking. Your success depends on which you use. Heads you win, tails you lose!"

"NO" PEOPLE AND "NOW" PEOPLE

Here is a three letter word that can mean the difference between success and failure. It can give you instant motivation anytime you think of it.

The word is *Now*.

The personnel manager of a large advertising agency was talking about one of his employees. "Tom is hopeless," he told me. "His mail stacks up for weeks. His phone messages go unanswered. His desk looks like the work of vandals."

Even Tom's secretary had given up.

After repeated suggestions that went unheeded, he was asked to look for a new job.

But Tom could have saved his position by practicing a simple daily plan of action. It's the "Now" approach. Anyone can use it.

The "Now" plan is simply this. Every time a piece of paper comes to your attention, do one of three things with it immediately: (1) Throw it away; (2) Take action on it; and (3) File it.

You'll be amazed to see how organized your life can seem when it becomes a habit.

Here's what Thomas Huxley tells you, "Perhaps the most valuable result of all education is the ability to make yourself do the thing you have to do, when it ought to be done whether you like it or not. It is the first lesson that ought to be learned."

Go ahead. Grab a project and see it through to completion.

Go ahead. Say "yes" or "no" rather than postponing a decision.

Go ahead. Answer that letter you have been dreading.

Put a little "Now" in your day. Go ahead!

The biggest difference between "No" people and "Now" people is their ability to get things done. Life's "losers" are those whose motto is: "Why do today what you can do tomorrow?" And they put off responsibility until it is suddenly too late.

But those who make it a habit of winning, also make it a habit to take immediate action. They not only plan their work—*they do it!*

Tackle That Tough Job

Are you a list maker? Millions of people are. They make grocery lists, party lists, and the list goes on.

The most popular list, however, is one called "Things to do today." I have made that a daily habit for years.

But recently I began to notice a recurring pattern. one or two major tasks would pop up on the list day after day. They simply wouldn't get done. Things like, "Clean the attic," or "Balance the checking account." I found myself writing them on the new list every morning.

What was the problem?

To find out, I pulled a crumpled list from the wastebasket and retraced my activities. And the discovery I made was remarkable.

Each day I started with the easiest, quickest, and most enjoyable task on my list. Then, as the day progressed and my energy was fading, I was just too tired to tackle the tough jobs. So they were postponed.

Here's how I cured the "list" problem. Instead of starting with the "pleasure" tasks, I rewrote the list in an order of "difficulty." The most time-consuming "tough" item was scheduled first. That's when I had the most energy. Then, as the tasks became shorter and more enjoyable, I sustained my energy since I was doing something I really liked.

Try it. *Right now, tackle that tough job on your list. You'll feel great the rest of the day!*

The Time Is Right

You can spend months, and even years, preparing for the future. I've known young adults who have such a fear of facing the "real world" that they become "professional students" and hide within the walls of a college for as long as possible. I talked to one fellow who was twenty-seven. He started college at eighteen and was still at it—*full time!*

But the philosopher Epicurus said, "The fool does not so much live as always get ready to live, and then one day it is too late."

If you are waiting for perfect conditions to get started, you may be waiting forever. Stop staring at the circumstances and begin working on the task ahead.

"He who watches the wind will not sow and he who looks at the clouds will not reap" (Ecclesiastes 11:4).

Don't hide in a corner waiting until the time is right. Don't procrastinate with the excuse that you're waiting for "God's will."

His will is clear. The Great Commission says "*Go!*"

Not next week. *Now!*

I remember hearing it said that, "It's difficult to turn the wheels of a parked automobile. But get it moving and you can guide it with just a touch."

That's power steering! And you can feel it when you begin moving toward your goal.

Don't wait. Get started *"Now!"*

LIVING THE YES YES LIFE

Several years ago, I began to study the lives of positive people. And at the same time I began writing down my observations and making notes that have found their way into these pages.

I have come to one conclusion: It is possible to live a *total* Yes Yes life!

I'm not talking about "thinking good thoughts" when it is convenient. I'm talking about a life style that encompasses *every thing you do.*

You *are* living in a No No world. And the same problems face the man of faith and the man of fear. But in *every* situation, you can exhibit Yes Yes living.

And there will come a time when it is more than a learned, practiced, deliberate response. It will become as natural as breathing or blinking. You won't even think about it. It will become YOU!

Like crossing the international date line, *it's a brand new day.* Perhaps it has already happened as you have read this book. Or perhaps you've been moving this direction slowly and you've just decided to declare once and for all time, "I'm finished with the No No world."

Here's What Makes It Easy

Once you've made your declaration, something quite extraordinary will start to work in your behalf! You'll find that total Yes Yes living is much easier than you thought, because *people will expect it of you.*

When you get the reputation of "someone who always sees the bright side," you'll take great pride in *keeping* it that way.

Yes, there will be those who will hurt your feelings. Yes, you will know physical pain. Yes, you'll make major blunders along the way. And yes, you'll be faced with financial problems.

But what a difference in the way you will react to those problems. You won't always laugh at them, but you won't be crying either. You'll respond with the calm assurance that God has things in control—and that you are His child. Even death, the ultimate tragedy, is not the end—but rather the beginning of eternity.

And there's another conclusion I have reached: *It is impossible to live the Yes Yes life without a strong faith in God.*

The "Greatest Commandment" is also the greatest gift. When you love God "with all your heart" you'll know joy beyond measure. And people will be able to tell the difference.

What a Way to Start the Day!

Let me tell you about a junior executive who arrived at 8:00 A.M. and said, "I must see the boss."

His secretary replied, "He's busy just now."

With that, he walked past her and opened the office door. To his astonishment, there was the executive, on his knees, quietly praying.

The young man backed out of the office and quietly closed the door. Then he said to the secretary. "Does he do this often?"

She said, "That's the way he always starts the day."

The junior executive said, "Then no wonder I always come to him for advice."

Yes, there is a distinct difference in the lives of those who have a strong spiritual foundation.

And there's another great transformation that takes place when you say goodbye to the "old you." Instead of dwelling on your own problems, *you'll be thinking of ways to help somebody else.*

You don't have to join the Rotary Club to practice their motto: "Service Above Self." It will become automatic as you start giving instead of taking.

The world is filled with those who give—but they do it grudgingly, even selfishly. Like the man who complained to his pastor about the church asking for money. He fumed, "This business of Christianity is just one continuous give, give, give."

The pastor thought for a moment and replied, "I want to thank you for one of the best definitions of Christianity I have ever heard."

Yes, *giving will become your way of life.*

It's Just the Beginning!

At the start of this book I pointed out that Yes Yes living goes beyond positive thinking. We have been talking about more than your mind—we've been talking about your *life!* Your actions. Your speaking. Your dealings with people.

And there's one theme I've talked about more than any other: It's not enough to think about an objective or believe in it, *you've got to do something about it!*

Yes Yes living requires *action!* It requires *work!* And it must be done *now!*

What are the characteristics of Yes Yes living? There are so many: Commitment, contentment, vision, laughter, goals, action, expectation, encouragement, persistence, and love. *But the greatest of these is love.*

When you have finished this book I am asking you to pause for a moment and have a heart to heart talk with yourself.

I am asking you to make a declaration that starting this very moment, the things in your life that should be changed, *will* be changed.

Find a place alone and speak these words out loud. Make them *your* words.

> Right now I am making a personal commitment to begin living the Yes Yes life. No matter what may be the problem I will face today or tomorow, I will not complain. Everything I say and do will be uplifting— both to me and to those I meet. I will never lose sight of my goal and I will achieve it because I expect to, because I will work, and because I will never give up. And I am making a personal commitment to keep the Greatest Commandment—to love God with all my heart.

Welcome to Yes Yes living!

If something contained in this book has had an effect on your life, I'd love to hear about it. With your permission, I'd like to share it as a brief example in a forthcoming book so your experience can be of help to others. You may write:

Neil Eskelin
Box 3155
Springfield, Missouri 65804